HOCKEYTOWN IN HIGH DEF

The Detroit Red Wings 2008 Championship Season in Photos

The Detroit News detnews.com

SPECIAL COMMEMORATIVE EDITION

Triumph Books and colophon are registered
trademarks of Random House, Inc.

Content packaged by Mojo Media, Inc.
Joe Funk: Editor
Jason Hinman: Creative Director

This book is available in quantity at special discounts for your group
or organization. For further information, contact:

Triumph Books
542 South Dearborn Street
Suite 750
Chicago, Illinois 60605
(312) 939-3330
Fax (312) 663-3557

Printed in United States of America
ISBN: 978-1-60078-179-7

Photos by David Guralnick, John Greilick, Dan Mears, and Dale Young.
Stories by Ted Kulfan, Bob Wojnowski, John Niyo, Vartan Kupelian, and Eric Lacy.
Edited by Ruben Luna, Brian Handley, Matt Charboneau, and Joe Adams.
Photo editing by Bob Houlihan.

CONTENTS

Stanley Cup Finals............................6
Conference Quarterfinals 22
Conference Semifinals.....................28
Conference Finals..........................34
Masterminds of Hockeytown.............40
Man in the Mirror 52
Player Bios..................................56
Superscout 104
Franzen 108
Brat Pack....................................112
Hometown...................................118
Lidstrom's Legend 122
Seeing Cleary 128
Kronwall of Pain 132
Chelios Churning 136
Stats 142

STANLEY CUP FINALS

By Bob Wojnowski

CHAMPS AGAIN

Team's experience returns glory to Detroit

They had waited long enough and skated hard enough, endured sudden turns and crushing twists, until finally, finally, the Red Wings went ahead and took what they had to have, what they've been chasing all year, what they always believed was theirs.

They took it in gasping, grasping fashion — fitting fashion, really — with Chris Osgood swiping at Pittsburgh's final, desperate shot. As the puck slid past the open goal, the crowd shrieked and the horn sounded, and there was the briefest pause to see if it really was over.

It was. And then it began, and now it begins. The Wings leaped on the ice in celebration-exhilaration-exhaustion, and launched another rollicking Detroit summer.

In another terrific showcase of drama, the Wings beat the Penguins, 3–2, on Wednesday to win the Stanley Cup. They took this Cup with cool force, in their classically composed way, rolling into an enemy arena and quelling the noise. And in case anyone still wondered, yes it's true: What's old is new again, and the hockey world is back to Red again.

They had to shake off smothering pressure and pesky Penguins to do it, but the Wings did it with great defense and stellar goaltending by Osgood, with the relentlessness of stars Henrik Zetterberg,

Pavel Datsyuk, and Nicklas Lidstrom, with pieces and poise from all areas.

They did it with a clinching third-period goal by Zetterberg, whose shot dribbled between the legs of goaltender Marc-Andre Fleury. The puck just sat there, for a second, two seconds, forever it seemed, until Fleury fell on it and knocked it in, and knocked the Penguins out.

From there, it all came spilling out, all the pent-up emotion and ramped-up talent, all the ingredients that made the Wings the best in hockey, and one of the most complete teams we've seen. As the game ended, that crushing three-overtime loss in Game 5 became just another obstacle hurdled, another piece of history.

"This is much more gratifying," said owner Mike Ilitch, comparing it to previous titles. "I'm not saying the (NHL salary cap) is because of us, but everybody wanted a fair shot. People expected us to go down."

The quiet stars

And now they know: History always reprises itself, and so do the Wings. They shook awake old glory, winning their fourth Cup in 11 years, their first in six years — Hockeytown reborn, or revisited.

Red Wings owner Mike Ilitch raises the Stanley Cup as his team joins the celebration.
John T. Greilick/The Detroit News

There were the new stars, similar to the previous stars, aligning themselves as they have throughout this dominating season. One by one, they hoisted the Stanley Cup, and with it, they raised the banner of a new era, the first championship without Steve Yzerman as captain or Scotty Bowman as coach.

There was another humble, superb leader in Nicklas Lidstrom, raising the Cup for the fourth time, his first as captain. He also becomes the first European captain to win the Cup.

"I watched Steve Yzerman hoist it three times, and I'm very proud of being the first European," Lidstrom said. "So much history with this team, the great tradition; I'm just so very proud."

Lidstrom lifted the Cup first, then handed it to the grizzled veteran, Dallas Drake, who had never won it, but symbolized the Wings' mix of young and old, stars and role players.

There, skating with the Cup, was another quiet superstar duo in Zetterberg and Datsyuk, who teamed up beautifully. Zetterberg won the Conn Smythe Trophy as playoff MVP, setting a franchise record for points in one postseason, eclipsing the mark shared by Yzerman and Sergei Fedorov.

"I've lost the words," a hoarse Zetterberg said. "Just an unbelievable feeling. When I saw Nick lifting the Cup, a great feeling went all through my body."

There was another stoic coach, Mike Babcock,

(above) Red Wings goaltender Chris Osgood makes the final save on a shot from Penguins all-star Sidney Crosby. Time expired before Marian Hossa's shot went wide on the rebound.
John T. Greilick/The Detroit News
(opposite) Chris Chelios, celebrating his third championship and second with the Wings, hands the Stanley Cup to Conn Smythe winner Henrik Zetterberg. Daniel Mears/The Detroit News

who had kept it all in, never distracted, rarely emotional, until finally he achieved what he was brought here to do.

There was Osgood, 10 years removed from his 1998 championship with the Wings, withstanding the heat to lift the Cup again, and lifting so many outdated labels with it. He was excellent in these playoffs, stepping in for Dominik Hasek during a dangerous first round and calmly restoring order.

"I think I got a bigger heart than people realize," Osgood said. "That's why I'm here, because I don't give up."

Once they started skating and firing, shaking off nerves and that devastating loss, the Wings knew exactly where they were headed, straight to the net, straight to the lead, straight to the podium and their favorite trophy. They took a slight detour around Fleury and Sidney Crosby, worthy opponents. But on the final night, the Wings proved themselves, one more time, to be unstoppable.

On opposition ice

They encountered trouble occasionally, especially in the first round, when the Predators tied the series 2–2 and ousted Hasek. From there, they were virtually unstoppable, finishing off the Predators, sweeping the Avalanche, outlasting the Stars in six games, then wearing down the young Penguins in six.

The Wings closed every series on the opposition's ice, and if that isn't the perfect example of experience and guts and resolve, nothing is. The Wings were coming off, arguably, the toughest loss in franchise history, the triple-overtime crusher that put the champagne back on ice and the Cup back in the box.

Could they get back up? Silly question. Of course they could.

Red Wings defensemen Brad Stuart, left, and Niklas Kronwall give Ryan Malone a rude welcome during the first period of Game 6.
John T. Greilick/The Detroit News

Valtteri Filppula, one of the Red Wings'
emerging stars, enjoys a champagne
bath in the dressing room after Game 6.
David Guralnick/The Detroit News

In the end, the Wings were the far-superior team, they just had to show it again, and they showed it quickly. Barely five minutes into the game, Brian Rafalski took a pass from Zetterberg, who was falling to the ice, and whistled a shot over Fleury's left shoulder for a 1–0 lead, which the Wings never relinquished.

Poise? They needed all of it, fighting off penalties, fighting off one last Pittsburgh flurry, when Crosby's final shot skittered toward Osgood, but not past him.

What exactly did we see during this relentless march to the Cup, during a regular season when the Wings were the NHL's best? Turns out, these Wings are every bit as good as promised, and maybe better than ever. They certainly belong in the discussion with the 1997, 1998, and 2002 champions.

A European captain

This is a team as diverse and complex as the city it represents, with players from all countries, all statuses, and all ages, with stars and role players. Much is made of the Wings' foreign influence, of the Swedes and Czechs and Russians and Canadians, with the occasional Fin thrown in.

Lidstrom is firmly entrenched as one of the greatest players in history, while obliterating the notion European players don't crave the Cup as much. What utter nonsense that turned out to be. From foreign roots, the Wings brought familiar traits — hard work, selflessness, and humility. Has a team this good ever been so unassuming? Have superstars this good — Lidstrom, Zetterberg, and Datsyuk — ever been so mild-mannered and maniacally competitive at the same time?

(above) Brian Rafalski, left, celebrates with Nicklas Lidstrom after Rafalski's goal put the Red Wings up 1–0 in the first period of Game 1. David Guralnick/The Detroit News
(opposite) The Red Wings mob goaltender Chris Osgood as they celebrate the 11th Stanley Cup in franchise history. Daniel Mears/The Detroit News

This was the night when the new faces of the Wings were fully revealed, when Babcock did what Bowman once did, when Lidstrom did what Yzerman once did.

This was the night when a new era was stamped with authenticity, when dominance was celebrated all over again. Eras are now bridged, and by doing so, the franchise proved it can win under any circumstances and any rules, with a salary cap or without.

Remember, the 2002 star-studded championship team was supposed to be the end of this craziness. The NHL went through a lockout to rein in spending, and big-money teams like the Wings were supposed to be doomed. The $80 million payroll was sliced in half, and the smartest front office in hockey — from Ilitch to Jimmy Devellano to Ken Holland to Jim Nill to Bowman — went to work.

Datsyuk and Zetterberg tied it all together but it begins with Lidstrom, who at 38, shows no signs of slowing down. In many ways, he's like the team itself, replacing ridiculous labels — too old, too soft — with poise and skill.

And speaking of dumb labels, all those knocks that the Wings couldn't handle the toughest games? Never to be heard again.

The Wings won the toughest games imaginable, deep into the spring, deep into the nights. As the pressure kept growing, they kept rebounding, and it's pretty simple with this remarkable team. There seldom are fiery speeches, or singularly super-human efforts. It's a collective thing, as it always has been, as it is again.

History reprised, glory restored. Oh, yes, hockey is back to Red again, and Stanley is headed to an old familiar home. ●

Marc-Andre Fleury, Brooks Orpik, and Hal Gill block Red Wings forward Tomas Holmstrom in the second period of Game 5.
David Guralnick/The Detroit News

Dan Cleary screens goaltender Marc-Andre Fleury in the third period of Game 5.
David Guralnick/The Detroit News

The Red Wings gather for a picture with the Cup. It was the 11th championship for the team and fourth in the last 11 seasons.
David Guralnick/The Detroit News

CONFERENCE QUARTERFINALS
By Bob Wojnowski

SHUTOUT
cements Osgood's position as No. 1 goalie

Thank goodness that's over. It was getting tedious. And redundant. And really, the Red Wings were firing so many shots, accurately or not, it was getting pointless.

The Wings wore down poor, battered Nashville by skating them into slush, but the bigger key was the Wings didn't wear themselves down. They completed a first-round ousting of the Predators with a 3–0 victory in Game 6, and for a series that sometimes seemed needlessly tight, it sure was useful.

By the end, the Wings were quicker in every way — to the puck, to the net, to the next round. In fact, as they head toward a possible matchup with old rival Colorado, the Wings are showing familiar and important signs, ones we'd waited to see.

And no, we're not just talking about Nicklas Lidstrom's shot from beyond center ice, which bounced past Nashville's pesky Dan Ellis for the game's first goal. Astute Wingologists will recall Lidstrom scored on a similar shot in the first round against Vancouver in 2002, righting a series the Wings trailed 2–0 and spurring an eventual Stanley Cup championship.

Oops. Let's not turn omens into mountains. There are no divine signs this time of year.

The Wings outshot the Predators ridiculously again, 43–20, and at some point, they'll need to cash in more often. But this was a good series for the Wings partly because Chris Osgood showed terrific poise replacing Dominik Hasek in net, and also because they faced just enough adversity against Nashville and weathered it all.

"They played us real hard," said Osgood, who stopped 53 of 54 shots after replacing Hasek. "The biggest thing I take away from this is, although we were getting a lot of chances and it was still only 1–0, we never deviated from our game plan. We're sticking with what we know. In the past, we might have gotten anxious and given up a breakaway or a two-on-one. That bodes well for us."

Positive signs

Things can change quickly, but the Wings are in better shape now than when the playoffs began. Once they solved the mid-series breakdowns by Hasek and the defense, they accomplished pretty much everything they wanted.

They won an overtime game. They overcame the

Red Wings goaltender Chris Osgood makes a third-period save in Game 6.
John T. Greilick/The Detroit News

"The reality is, if you get through the first round, it takes a weight off and you can just play."

Osgood as ever

For certain, Osgood is better for it. It's impossible to overstate how tricky that transition was, and how clutch he truly was. Did he dive from post to post and grab pucks out of mid-air? No. Did he make every key save, except one late in Game 5? Yep.

"He looked really relaxed, and that gives the whole team confidence," Lidstrom said. "Once we got deeper into the series, we played a lot better defense. Now I think we're in a good groove."

When the going got tight, the Wings got tighter — in the right way. But the next opponent will have many more weapons than Nashville, and this series should serve as a warning. Osgood will be challenged far more severely.

frustration of a hot opposing goalie. They didn't suffer any significant injuries and saw solid improvement from four of their own ailing players — Mikael Samuelsson, Valtteri Filppula, Dan Cleary, and Brad Stuart. Young players such as Jiri Hudler and Darren Helm showed promise.

Oh yes, and the Wings found their goalie. Osgood wasn't tested a ton but he was oh-so-good when needed, and that's all he has to be. Mike Babcock confirmed the obvious, that Osgood would remain in net. And then the coach practically gushed (for him, anyway) about how the Wings encountered danger and shoved it aside.

"I thought we got better, and we should just get better and better as the playoffs go on," Babcock said.

If this goes the way it should for a No. 1 seed, the Wings will get stronger. Now that Osgood has a couple of games under his pads, he could get even stronger.

"I always said I was ready," Osgood said. "I think the whole team stayed composed. It was an in-the-trenches kind of series, and we were good in the trenches."

They were good in many places, eventually. They reacted well to legitimate concern. They handled themselves physically.

To keep advancing, the Wings will have to keep getting better. This was a start, packed with decent signs. The first-round pressure is off. The real telling stuff is about to begin. ●

(above) Chris Osgood makes a second-period save against the Tampa Bay Lightning at Joe Louis Arena. David Guralnick/The Detroit News
(opposite) Tomas Holmstrom celebrates with teammate Pavel Datsyuk after scoring a third-period goal in Game 2 against Nashville. David Guralnick/The Detroit News

Red Wings center Johan Franzen charges between Predators defensemen Ryan Suter and Greg de Vries, but goaltender Dan Ellis makes the save. David Guralnick/The Detroit News

CONFERENCE SEMIFINALS

By Ted Kulfan

AVALANCHE
under Red Wings' landslide

This time there was no Patrick Roy in net, and it was Denver rather than Joe Louis Arena.

This wasn't a Game 7, either, but a rather anticlimactic Game 4.

But the Red Wings hammered the Colorado Avalanche in a series-clinching game again, this time 8–2, to sweep the Western Conference semifinal series in four games.

And it was every bit the rout the final score indicated.

Johan Franzen led the way, scoring three goals, giving him nine for the series (Franzen has 11 in the playoffs).

The nine goals are a Red Wings record for a four-game series, breaking Gordie Howe's eight goals in seven games in 1949.

Franzen's 11 goals also set a Wings record for a playoff year. Peter Klima (10 goals, 1988), Sergei Fedorov (10 goals in 22 games, 1998), and Brett Hull (10 goals in 23 games, 2002) were the previous record-holders.

"Every time you get mentioned with him (Gordie Howe), it's a great honor," Franzen said. "I don't know what to say. I feel real lucky right now."

How good was Franzen in this series, and how ineffective were the Avalanche? The Avs also finished the series with nine goals.

"It's not often you see a player score like this, it's fun to be part of it," said Henrik Zetterberg, who had two goals and two assists Thursday. "I'm real happy for him. He's been working hard."

The Wings flew back to Detroit on Friday morning and await the winner of the Dallas–San Jose series. Dallas leads the series 3–1.

This will be the Wings' second consecutive trip to the Western Conference finals. They lost to Anaheim in six games last season.

"I'm thrilled," coach Mike Babcock said. "We're going to have an opportunity. At this point last year we were playing pretty good, but it's hard. But Mule (Franzen) is a better player, (Dan) Cleary is a better player, Fil (Valtteri Filppula) is a better player, (Niklas) Kronwall is a better player. We may be better. We'll find out."

The Wings realize they're only halfway where they want to be and what they want to achieve.

"It's good, it's an accomplishment, but we have a lot of work to do," goalie Chris Osgood said. "We realize how hard it's been to get to this position and how hard it's going to be going forward. We have to be real focused on our game plan. We

Darren McCarty, who returned to the Wings late in the season after being signed as a free agent, gets into a tussle with Cody McCormick in the second period of Game 1.
David Guralnick/The Detroit News

28

can't deviate from the game plan."

Franzen and Zetterberg weren't the only offensive stars.

Mikael Samuelsson had two goals. Pavel Datsyuk had three assists. Nicklas Lidstrom, Valtteri Filppula, and Jiri Hudler each had two assists. Tomas Holmstrom had the other goal.

The Wings chased Avalanche goalie Jose Theodore for the third time in the four-game series. Theodore allowed goals to Holmstrom and Franzen 47 seconds apart late in the first period giving the Wings a 3–1 lead after one period.

Theodore allowed three goals on 15 shots and was replaced by Peter Budaj.

The Wings were without defenseman Chris Chelios (lower body injury), scratched just after warm-ups concluded.

"Cheli should be ready for the next round," Babcock said. "He couldn't get his legs going. I'm pretty sure he'll be ready."

Andreas Lilja replaced Chelios in the lineup.

The demoralized Avalanche were without Peter Forsberg (groin), Ryan Smyth (foot), Paul Stasny (knee), and Wojtek Wolski (upper body), four of their leading scorers.

Tyler Arnason and former Michigan State defenseman John-Michael Liles scored power play goals for the Avalanche.

"Their team was depleted," Babcock said. ●

Colorado goaltender Jose Theodore looks back at the puck in the net after Johan Franzen scores in the first period of Game 1.
David Guralnick/The Detroit News

Johan Franzen joins the Joe Louis Arena fans
in cheering Daniel Cleary's first-period goal in
Game 1. David Guralnick/The Detroit News

CONFERENCE FINALS

By John Niyo

SAVING FACE
Red Wings regain composure, win Game 6

They came back to retrieve the item they'd left behind.

And this morning, the Red Wings head home with one trophy in tow and their sights firmly set on another.

The Wings dispatched the Dallas Stars, 4–1, in Game 6 of the Western Conference finals at American Airlines Center. Now they're headed back to the Stanley Cup Finals for the fourth time in a dozen years, and the first since winning the championship in 2002.

"It feels real good," owner Mike Ilitch said after sharing a laugh with team vice president Steve Yzerman in the hallway outside the Wings' jubilant dressing room. "It's been five years, but it feels like 15 since we were in the Finals.

"(The critics) didn't expect us to be up there this year. They were looking for us to go down. So that makes it extra special."

The marquee matchup the NHL had hoped for — Detroit versus Pittsburgh in the Stanley Cup Finals — finally is here.

"It's going to be a lot of fun," said Wings coach

Mike Babcock, who already was trying to paint his team as the underdog. "I mean, they're 12–2 in the playoffs. I think we're 12–4, aren't we? So, I mean, they've been better than us."

Time will tell, but the Wings clearly were the best in the West. And the finish to the conference finals looked a lot like the start. Both games ended in 4–1 routs, and true to form on Monday, the team that scored first won, just as it had the five previous games.

After a poor start at home Saturday, the Wings wasted little time in Game 6, grabbing a 1–0 lead at 3:45 of the opening period after a fluttering centering pass from Dallas Drake hit Draper squarely in the mouth. Draper, who'd gained the inside position at the far post behind the Stars' Mike Ribeiro, took a swipe at the loose puck with his stick, but it already had trickled into the net behind a surprised Marty Turco.

"I felt it right away, but I still saw the puck and saw it go in," said Draper, who immediately headed to the dressing room, where he received six stitches in his lip and a brace for three loose teeth. "Who cares? It hit my chin and went in. It'll be all right."

Dallas goaltender Marty Turco reaches back to keep the puck out of the net in the second period of Game 5. David Guralnick/The Detroit News

By the time he'd returned with about seven minutes left in the period, the Wings were up 2–0 on a power-play goal by Pavel Datsyuk. The Wings had just killed off a Stars power play when defenseman Trevor Daley drew an interference penalty holding up Datsyuk in front of the Stars' bench.

Datsyuk scored on a rebound off Nick Lidstrom's point shot at 11:41 of the period, prying the puck out from under defenseman Nicklas Grossman's skates while he and Sergei Zubov were preoccupied with Tomas Holmstrom in front of the net.

"We drove the net hard early, and we were rewarded," Babcock said.

The Wings put things out of reach on a fluky mistake by Turco late in the first. Thinking he'd gloved the puck safely on a shot by Brett Lebda, Turco rose to his feet only to discover the puck was in his pads.

Drake was right there to slam the rebound in for a 3–0 lead at 16:17. It was Drake's first goal of the postseason — actually, it was his first in the playoffs since April 12, 2004 — and it all but secured the 16-year NHL veteran's first trip to the Stanley Cup Finals.

"It's a huge thrill for me," Drake said. "It's really gratifying to contribute when you can."

Zetterberg's short-handed breakaway goal — he intercepted a bad pass by Stars captain Brenden Morrow at center ice — turned the game into a rout at 3:11 of the second period.

Stephane Robidas' power-play goal at 2:27 of the third period spoiled Chris Osgood's shutout bid. But Osgood, who broke Terry Sawchuk's franchise record with his 48th career playoff victory in a Red Wings uniform, had to make 15 saves as the Stars — with a little help from the referees — refused to lay down in the final 20 minutes.

"We didn't want to have any regrets," Morrow said. "We went out and played a heck of a third period. We just started a little late tonight."

In the series, too. But the fun is just beginning in Detroit.

"We've got a good team," Ilitch said. "It's better than I thought. I think Nick (Lidstrom) has done a wonderful job as captain, they've got good chemistry, and they play hard. What else can you say?" ●

(above) Stars defenseman Mattias Norstrom and Wings forward Tomas Holmstrom battle for position during the third period of Game 5. David Guralnick/The Detroit News
(opposite) Wings defenseman Brett Lebda flies into Stars left wing Brad Winchester along the boards during the second period of Game 2. John T. Greilick/The Detroit News

Jiri Hudler scores against Stars goaltender Marty Turco
on a power play in the first period of Game 5.
David Guralnick/The Detroit News

MASTERMINDS OF HOCKEYTOWN

A preseason roundtable discussion with Red Wings' leadership

Together, they have 101 years experience with the same team and own 25 Stanley Cup rings. Together, they've built and maintained a franchise that has weathered the NHL's titanic changes and withstood the forces of parity.

This isn't about what the Red Wings will do this season, or what they did last season.

This is about a remarkable 25-year arc that began in 1982 when Mike Ilitch bought a sad-sack team, hired a hotshot executive named Jimmy Devellano and began assembling a brain trust that continues to grow and evolve and win.

Ilitch has owned the team for 25 years, and Devellano has been with him for all 25. Ken Holland has been here 24 years, the last 10 as general manager. Consultant Scotty Bowman has been here 14 years, including nine as coach, winning the Stanley Cup three times. Assistant general manager Jim Nill has been here 13 years.

Together, the group represents continuity you almost never see anymore, a link also reflected in the long career of Steve Yzerman, now making the transition from the ice to the front office. Continuity is a major reason the Wings hold the longest streak of consecutive playoff appearances — 16 and counting — of any franchise in the four major professional sports.

Hailed by many, railed by some, the Wings have acquired labels over the years ranging from "underachievers" to "visionaries," from "arrogant" to "brilliant." In a rare, candid glimpse into the inner workings of hockey's most successful brain trust, all five executives sat in Ilitch's Joe Louis Arena suite recently with the *News'* Ted Kulfan, John Niyo, and Bob Wojnowski for an animated 90-minute conversation.

News: It's easy to look at it today and see what you've built. But I wonder, going back 25 years to when you bought a team that people called the Dead Things, if you could've envisioned 'Hockeytown?'

Jim Nill, assistant general manager; Jim Devellano, senior vice president/alternate governor; Mike Ilitch, owner; Ken Holland, general manager; and Scotty Bowman, former coach/advisor. David Guralnick/The Detroit News

Ilitch: No, I couldn't. But I was pretty cocky.... I realized it was a wonderful opportunity, and timing was on my side. With Mr. (Bruce) Norris, they'd hit bottom. There was a lot of bad publicity about them. And he and Gordie (Howe) got into it a little bit, so I got a bargain deal.

You need timing and luck. And I got very lucky. But I thought we were gonna tear it up until I got a hold of Jimmy (Devellano). (Laughter.) When I hired him, he told me, 'Settle down.'

Devellano: I said, 'This is gonna take time — probably a little more than both of us would like.'

News: Jimmy was your most important hire. What struck you about him?

Ilitch: Well, I couldn't make up my mind. And I'd run out of places to go, I'd run out of conversation. So here I am driving (with Devellano) around Cranbrook, saying, 'I want to show you where my kids go to school.' I was that hard-up for things to

talk about. I like to get that instinct, that feel, and I couldn't get it. So I strung it out for a couple days. I know he got tired of driving.

Devellano: Well, it was the funniest interview process I think anybody's ever been through.... He took me to a Wendy's franchise, and I thought, 'What am I doing going to a Wendy's?' I'm back in the kitchen seeing how they're flipping the hamburgers. And then he takes me to Little Caesars and takes me into the room where all the cheese and the dough is. And I thought, 'Well, if I don't get this job, at least I'm gonna know a little bit about the fast-food industry.' (Laughter.)

News: Jimmy, the notion of starting from the ground up: That didn't give you pause?

Devellano: I had a goal. I wanted to become a general manager. It was very, very important to me.

Now, the bad news was that the team was really in the Detroit River. I mean, really in the Detroit River. In a 21-team league (where 16 teams made the playoffs), this team had missed the playoffs in 14 of the previous 16 years. Now I don't know how you do that. But somehow they did.

News: I'm guessing Mr. Ilitch was saying 'Win now' and you were always preaching, 'Let's build it slowly?'

Devellano: Our philosophies were a little different. You have to remember where both people were coming from. I was coming from a hockey background with the Islanders, having done it through the draft, and I understood it would take time and we needed to be patient.

Ken Holland, general manager; Scotty Bowman, former coach/advisor; Mike Ilitch, owner; Jim Devellano, senior vice president/alternate governor; and Jim Nill, assistant general manager. David Guralnick/The Detroit News

Mr. Ilitch is an entrepreneur. He's a guy that wants things done quickly. He was able to do that in his business. And to be fair, I had to think a little bit like him, too, because (we only had) 2,100 season tickets on July 12, 1982. So there was some sense of urgency. We had to try to build for the future, but we also had to create some kind of buzz here.

News: Do you recall what your payroll was back then?

Ilitch (motioning to Devellano): He knows.

Devellano: Yeah, the first year I was here, our payroll was $2.8 million for the whole team.

News: The innovation — signing college players, going into Russia and drafting the European players — if we're looking for a secret ingredient, is that it?

Ilitch: Yeah, I think we've extended ourselves more than anybody else in the league. Don't take this the wrong way, but I think we have vision. I mean, we were trying to get players out of Russia when it was a communist country.

I remember when Sergei (Fedorov) was going to defect (in 1990) in Vancouver, I had a pilot for my plane and it was his first day on the job. And I said, 'I've got a player who's going to defect from Russia and you've gotta go pick him up.' His eyes got like saucers and he said, "I've got to go to Russia?!?!' And I said, 'No, no, no. Just Vancouver.' He was petrified — probably ready to quit right away.

Devellano: We all knew that Russia had a won-derful supply of hockey players. And Czechoslovakia, too. But you couldn't get the bug-gers out. But it bothered me when we'd be drafting in the third, fourth, fifth round and we'd be taking North American players and really our scouts weren't that high on them. Finally, in about '89, I

remember sitting with Kenny (Holland) and Neil Smith, who were our lead scouts at the time, and saying, "Who's the best 18-year-old player in the world?' They both said, 'Sergei Fedorov.'

Holland: And our question to Jimmy was, 'Are you prepared to waste a draft pick? Are you prepared to draft a player and never see him?' Jimmy said, 'Get the best player and we'll worry about that later.'

Ilitch: There were quite a few years I had to go to George Bush Sr., and go through distant political connections, to get to the embassies of all these other countries, trying to get players out. We're up at 3:30 AM talking to the embassies. We did a lot of work. When we got (Petr) Klima out, we had a double trunk (to) get him into Austria. He wouldn't go unless his girlfriend came. So we squeezed the girlfriend in the trunk, too.

News: A trunk?

Holland: The trunk of a car. He was going across the border. (Nick) Polano was over there. And he made some contacts and ultimately these people got Klima to defect. So they put Klima in a fake trunk and they drove across the border.

Ilitch: And I had a suitcase this big full of money that we sent over to get (Vladimir Konstantinov). I flew to Bulgaria to get the wife and the child, and then we got the money to him.... We got him discharged out of the Army.

News: Can you say how much cash?

Ilitch: No, I can't say how much. It was a lot of pizza coupons, let's put it that way. (Laughter)

News: When all this is going on, is anybody else in the league doing it?

Ilitch: No, they haven't got a clue.

Devellano: The one thing we always knew, and I

learned this 40 years ago from Scotty: You have to have the best players ... You couldn't get enough of them out of the draft with just North Americans. So we went into the European market and we were ahead of the curve.

News: You mentioned the '89 draft earlier, and I think that, as much as anything, was the cornerstone for what you guys built here ...

Devellano: Without a doubt.... Our first pick was Mike Sillinger. He still plays in the league — not a bad hockey player. No. 2 was Bob Boughner, who played in the NHL. No. 3 was (Nicklas) Lidstrom.... Fourth was Fedorov. Sixth round was Dallas Drake. The 11th round we got Konstantinov. For this franchise, it was a draft for the ages.

There's two drafts in the 26 years I've been here that really put us on the map. The first one was '83, and we got (Yzerman) by default by missing the playoffs. And then '89.

We're due, Kenny and Jimmy, for one more. (Laughter.)

News: The Cups started coming when Scotty got here. How did you guys land him?

Devellano: Mike Keenan had been kind of hovering around, wanting to get in here. And I'll make it brief: I just didn't feel he was the right person here for the organization. And I had a meeting with Mr. Ilitch because we were at a crisis. We felt that if we were gonna move the team forward and start to have some real playoff success, we had to get the best, most proven coach that there was. So I sat down with Mr. and Mrs. Ilitch and I said, 'Look, there's two people that ... are the very best in the business, that have (Stanley Cup) rings on both hands, and they both sort of think alike.' One was

Scotty Bowman, the other was Al Arbour. And Mr. Ilitch said, 'Go get one of them.'

Bowman: I got into a bit of a contract dispute (coaching the Penguins from 1991–93).... And Jimmy phoned me and asked whether I would ever be interested in coaching in Detroit. I talked with Pittsburgh, and I think if they had come through, I might not have come here. But then Jimmy said Mr. Ilitch wants to meet you.... We talked for about three hours — and I knew right away. We hadn't even talked contract. But Mike said, 'I really want this team to win. And I think you can pull it off. We want you to come. We'll do whatever it takes to win.'

Like Jimmy said, the team was on the threshold. They had a lot of good players, a lot of good young players, but just didn't play enough defense to win.

News: On that subject, how close was Steve Yzerman to being traded?

Devellano: There were talks. Steve Yzerman knows that. I've told him that. But as I told Stevie, even while it was going on, 'Look, Steve, if you're going to be dealt to Ottawa, we have to get something real good now to replace you and a whole lot more for the future.' Ottawa couldn't deliver on it. I don't even think they could pay the contract, could they, Scotty?

Bowman: No, I don't think so. I remember Jimmy saying, 'You're just spinning your wheels because Mike Ilitch would never trade Steve Yzerman.' And I remember Mike coming to me after my first year here — because Steve got injured that year — and saying, 'You haven't even seen what this guy can do.'

News: Did it ever come to your desk, Mr. Ilitch?

Ilitch: No, and I didn't want it to come.

Mike Ilitch

(Laughter.) I'd heard the rumblings, but ...

News: Do you feel like, over time, once 'Hockeytown' was built, that the NHL took advantage of you to a certain degree?

Ilitch: Well, I think they want to keep us in the division we're in now, because we fill their arenas. And I do think we're like the poor man's Yankees. They don't want to see us win anymore, because we've been up there so long.

Nill: I think that's what drives us almost. There's a new CBA put in place, everybody says we're gonna fall. I think internally we thought, 'You know what? We're gonna stay No. 1 no matter what. We're gonna show 'em.'

Devellano: Kenny Holland and I have been in the company of at least two general managers — and I won't tell you who they are — (who said), 'We can hardly wait until we have a salary cap so we're on a level playing field with you.' (They

were) intimating that once the salary cap is in place, they're going to come and pass us. Well, one team missed the playoffs last year, now that they're on an even playing field, and the other just about caught us but didn't quite do it.

But you know what? Isn't that how we feel about the Yankees? Don't we get tired of them — we want to bring the Yankees down?

I'd just like to add one more thing about expansion. There's little doubt that Vegas is coming in (as an expansion franchise) — it's about four years from now. And I truly believe (NHL commissioner) Gary Bettman will move us east at that time.

Ilitch: Bettman has told Jimmy and I on two or three occasions that we're next.

News: It has been two full seasons since the lockout. Can you guys assess the damage? Was it worth it, ultimately?

Devellano: I think it was necessary. I think it's healthy for the game overall. I know that Kenny and I and Jimmy Nill were scared (expletive) about the salary cap because, you know, maybe it would bring us down? We were going from $78 million down to $40 million? But two years out, it hasn't brought us down. And I think (teams like) Tampa, Atlanta, Phoenix — they have to have some cap on salaries.

Ilitch: I don't like it, though. I like going out and getting the players. (Laughter).

News: Did you take offense when people would say you were buying championships?

Ilitch: Oh, you do then. I guess the ones that

General manager Ken Holland takes part in a roundtable discussion about the team.
David Guralnick/The Detroit News

don't like it, they've got to have something bad to say about you.

Bowman: I think if you talk to people around the league now, though, they look at where some of the top players on the Red Wings were drafted, like (Pavel) Datsyuk and (Henrik) Zetterberg, and (Valtteri) Filppula now. They're starting to realize, and they're amazed where these players were drafted — third, fourth, fifth, and sixth rounds. I talk to a lot of people, and they say, 'How do they get all these players?'

News: You talked about scouting earlier. Jim (Nill), are you doing it differently than other teams?

Nill: I don't know if we're doing it differently than any other teams. Everybody's in Europe now. But we had to change our philosophy a little bit because we started trading away first-round picks and that.

News: Last year in the playoffs, when it was hard to sell tickets, was that a red flag for you?

Ilitch: It meant to us, wake up. Wake up. In other words, the price is too high and ... they're sick and tired of playing Nashville and Columbus and all those teams. And the exhibition games, getting charged for the exhibition games.

There's such a thing as being over-focused on winning and maybe being a little out of touch with the fans.

News: Do you think style of play, the way the NHL is now, factors into that?

Holland: I'd like to see more physical play. My personal feeling is from the top of the circle down, I'd like to see more of the old game. People want to see battles in the corner, battles in front of the net.

We've expressed that at the GM meetings.

Bowman: And the two-referee system, that's

another thing, too. It's in now, and it has taken the players awhile to adjust.... I don't think people want to see a game where there's 15 power plays.

Ilitch: Another subject, let me ask you guys a question: You see this new sport that's just come in where they kick each other — what do they call it?

News: Mixed martial arts?

Ilitch: That thing is really drawing. I mean, the guy that started that can sell it now for a billion dollars. The ratings are sky-high. So people like rough stuff. And Don Cherry and people like that over the years have been talking about, 'Let's take advantage of what we have.' We're the only sport that fights.... That gets to be something where it's real controversial between the league and the teams — a lot of opinions on it. But you get too conservative and too laid-back and you can see what happens.

News: Are they trying to placate the TV audience? Because why hasn't the NHL hit it on TV?

Devellano: It's still a regional sport.

Ilitch: But look at baseball. I can't talk this way in front of certain people. They were doing $1 billion, $1.25 billion (in revenue) and they go to interleague play and the wild card and they do over $5 billion. I mean, it's just a couple moves to create excitement, you know? And here we are locked into that (schedule) and it's like, 'We really hurt the sport.'

And then the guys that don't have guts, that use their sticks and everything? Well, it used to be the league ruled itself. You're a dirty player, you're gonna get it. (Bob) Probert's gonna go out there and kick your (expletive). Or the No. 1 fighter against the No. 1 fighter on each team, you know? But they've taken that away now.

News: You're just one of 30 in this league. Do you feel you can get things done, as an owner or through the board of governors?

Ilitch: To get things done, you've got to be strong politically. You've got to be active and make yourself popular with the other owners. You've got to call them on the phone, you've got to be going to dinner with them.

But the problem is, since 1994, I think it is, we've only got three original owners left. So all the owners are new in hockey. And I wish you guys could come to a meeting.

News: So do we. (Laughter)

Ilitch: There's not a lot said. Bettman got his training from the NBA, where (commissioner David) Stern runs it with an iron fist. And you've got all those billionaires in there (as NBA owners) and these guys come in like little puppies. (Stern) has got it all strategically worked out weeks and months before he goes into that meeting. These guys come ambling in and (Stern) really controls things.

Well, you can imagine (what it's like) having so many new owners in the league.

Devellano: It is very difficult in a 30-team league. When I started going to the owners meetings for Mr. Ilitch, it was a 21-team league and it was a little easier to be closer to people. Now, with 30 owners, every time I go to a meeting there's new people representing teams, a lot of non-hockey people, corporate people. Not to disparage them, but they don't know the game and the issues of the game.

So it is a little frustrating in order to get anything done. What Mr. Ilitch and I have tried to do is kind of pick our priorities. And we feel our priorities,

first of all, is to get our schedule changed. We want more Eastern Conference teams in this building, that's No. 1. Mr. Ilitch has worked through Gary Bettman and it's gonna happen.

News: It's definitely going to happen?

Devellano (sternly): It's going to happen.

The second thing, more quietly, behind the scenes, Mr. Ilitch, myself, Kenny, we've worked Gary one-on-one, and at some point, we've got to get in the East. And he has kind of said, 'Look, the league is going to change structure, meaning expansion, just leave it with me.'

Ilitch: Scotty, let me ask you a question: Has officiating changed at all since you've been in the game?

Bowman: Oh, yeah, it's much more structured now. Sometimes I wonder if referees should have the right to manage the game in some instances.

News: Mr. Ilitch, after 25, 26 years now, do you still live and die with each game and each season, or are you able to appreciate it more?

Ilitch: Oh, I appreciate the success. But you never get used to losing. It bothers you. You don't have a good day the next day. You talk yourself into it as much possible. You say, 'Come on, let's go, be a man, you win some, you lose some, what the hell's the matter with you?'

(Laughter.)

But I hate losing. I can't stand it. Baseball, the same way. Everybody competes and doesn't like to lose. But I've enjoyed it overall. I enjoy this relationship. I've enjoyed the success and I remember all of it vividly, the glory of it all.

News: What common trait do you think binds this group here?

Ilitch: Passion.

Nill: It's all about winning. We just want to win.

Holland: And we love the game. Even sitting at this table, I mean, it's been well-documented — Scotty has had an opportunity this summer and he could've left us. Jim Nill has had opportunities.

Ilitch: He's had everybody wanting him. Same thing with Kenny, they want you, they want Jimmy.

Devellano: The challenge of staying on top, especially when some people in our industry thought the cap would even things out and bring us down. It's been a tremendous driving force.

News: It's a challenge and a pressure. People were crushed last year when you lost to Anaheim. What about the pressure going into this year — you like this team's chances?

Ilitch: Oh, I do. I'll speak up. I think we've got a good team, we got a good shot at the Cup. Last year we should've won the Cup. We were 2–2 — and I'm gonna talk like a typical fan now — it was 2–2, and a minute and a half to go, and they called the cheapest penalty I've ever seen.

Showing their Stanley Cup rings are: (from left) Scotty Bowman, former coach/advisor; Ken Holland, general manager; Jim Nill, assistant general manager; Mike Ilitch, owner; and Jim Devellano, senior vice president/alternate governor. David Guralnick/The Detroit News

Devellano: Yeah, (expletive).

Bowman: Two-man system.

Ilitch: Now, and here's the big tears coming out, but prior to that, Kenny brought it to the league's attention, there was a flagrant penalty on Anaheim, right in front of the referee, and they didn't call it. Then they turned around and called that (interference) penalty (on Datsyuk). We had that game won, and we'd have been up 3–2 in the series.

That same referee in 1994, when we were down 3–2 going into Toronto, we score four power-play goals, we come back to Detroit 3–3, and the referee did not call one penalty — not one — during the game or overtime. So you figure that one out. We lost, and that's the same guy that made that call in this arena with a minute and a half to go.

News: After a season where you've lost, is there one message, Mr. Ilitch, you've been consistent on, one point you always make?

Ilitch: I'll just say it ad nauseam: 'Win.' That's all we talk about. 'Whatever it takes.' We've got a lot of pride, you know. This is a great city, they've really supported the team. We've got great fans. You know, this sounds corny, but I like the fact we're being recognized as the greatest sports city in the country. With all the problems we have, with the sad condition the state is in (and) the city is in. It's sports.

Now, with the Lions, I'm praying, I want the Lions to win. And if the Lions win, look what kind of city we'll have, as far as sports.

News: So the next big thing for the Wings is the arena situation, whether you renovate the Joe or build a new one.

Ilitch: Let me ask you guys a question. Do you think we should stay here or build a new arena?

News: I think you should build a new arena, but I'm not paying the bills. I've always felt this is a good place to watch a hockey game, I will say that.

Ilitch: Yeah. Well, we love these sightlines. We would take these same sightlines. But there's a lot of people saying, 'Why don't you stay at the Joe?'

News: So what's your timetable on a decision?

Ilitch: Let's go on to the next thing.

News: Besides the arena, what is the next big thing on the plate for the Wings — locking up Zetterberg to a long-term deal?

Holland: I think the challenge every year is to continue being an elite team, and that comes to drafting, developing, and then making the right decisions on who to keep and who to let go.

General manager Ken Holland joins a roundtable discussion about the team.
David Guralnick/The Detroit News

Ilitch: We gotta sign our players.

Holland: Zetterberg obviously is an unrestricted free-agent two years from now. He's a guy we want to keep. And having Datsyuk and Zetterberg, from a competitive standpoint, and obviously we want Nick Lidstrom to remain here. I think Nick can remain an elite defenseman for 3-4-5 more years, the way he trains and the way he plays. If you've got Lidstrom and Datsyuk and Zetterberg, you've got the nucleus of a good hockey team.

News: Does that mean you're committed to spending to the cap?

Holland: I'd say so.... (But) I don't think we want to spend money for the sake of spending money. Part of being below the cap this year was designed because we have so many people unrestricted.

Zetterberg is an unrestricted free agent in '09. Look at our team — three-quarters are probably unrestricted either in the summer of '08 or the summer of '09. We like a lot of our players, and we better be in a position to be able to commit to them. Now, would we like to be able to add one more real top player in either the summer of '08 or '09? ... If we can get a lot of these guys signed long-term and know where we're at, now maybe we can go get one more star player.

News: Touch on Steve (Yzerman) for a second. What's his role going forward? Is it still being defined?

Devellano: Steve and I and Mr. Ilitch used to have these talks, so when we finally sat down to try to figure out just how we could utilize a guy like Steve, the more we talked, the more we felt like, you know what, let's utilize him in every area that he would like to be involved in. Whether it be scouting, whether it be helping in Grand Rapids with the young players, whether it be marketing, maybe helping Mike Babcock with a certain problem player, or working with Kenny and Jimmy Nill on contracts.

We told Steve he can be as involved in every area of the franchise as he wants to be, and he can put in as much time as he feels he wants to. It's kind of evolving.

Holland: For Steve, it's how much time you can commit because there's a lot of down time, when not much is going on. But you need to be there every day, just to talk about things. Certainly, Steve can be right beside me.

Ilitch: He's happy, though. He loves it. And he could end up being an owner, too, one day. He might be part of a group one day, who knows?

News: It seems you've always got room for another brain in the brain trust.

Devellano: Absolutely. And you know, it's a little bit like what I've said about Scotty Bowman. Steve's presence means so much, his presence to the fans, to the players, to the coaching staff, to us. Just like Scotty, I think his presence just elevates our organization, I really do.

Ilitch: Because he cares so much.

News: So, Mr. Ilitch, after 25 years of all this, is it still as rewarding as when you were building way back when?

Ilitch: Yeah, it's just as much fun. I know it's not gonna go on forever, though. (Laughter.)

You know what, if you love sports, it keeps you alive, it keeps you vibrant. You got your buddies (he looks around the table). It's wonderful. I pinch myself a lot of times. ●

By John Niyo

MAN IN THE MIRROR
Belief in himself works for Babcock

It's okay to be a little starstruck. Even Mike Babcock was willing to admit that on the eve of the NHL All-Star Game as he started rattling off possible line combinations .

By virtue of the Wings' league-best record at midseason, Babcock was named to coach the Western Conference team, a group that boasts a combined 58 All-Star appearances, 15 Stanley Cup rings, two league most valuable player awards, two playoff MVPs, a pair of scoring titles, seven Norris Trophy (best defenseman) awards, and a half-dozen Olympic gold medals.

"Really, you just want to enjoy the experience, being around the greatest players in the world," said Babcock, in his third season in Detroit and his fifth as an NHL coach. "It should be a lot of fun. I'm excited just to sit back and watch."

But there was no time for stargazing in the summer of 2005, when Babcock landed what he now calls his "dream job" in Detroit, serving as the bench boss for one of the most successful franchises in professional sports.

"When you first come in here and you walk down that hall (in Joe Louis Arena), a lot of the players' names are up there on the wall — they're already enshrined here," said Babcock, noting the murals honoring the Wings championship teams from 1997, 1998, and 2002. "Those players, they're part of the fabric, they've been here. They're more important than me. So the question walking in is, 'What are you gonna do to help us win?'"

And yet, it's Babcock's answer that helps explains his inaugural All-Star visit. He insists now, and rather believably, he wasn't intimidated by the challenge he accepted in Detroit, or of coaching the likes of Steve Yzerman, Chris Chelios, and Nicklas Lidstrom.

"Not one bit," said Babcock, whose ties to the Wings organization actually date to 2000 when he coached a shared minor-league affiliate in Cincinnati. "And you know why it wasn't? Because over time, you build a foundation of success and your belief in that, and of your belief in yourself.

"That's the most important attribute for a head coach, especially in the NHL: It's confidence. If you don't have it, they can smell it a million miles away."

Coach Mike Babcock shouts out plays during the second period of Game 1 of the Stanley Cup Finals. David Guralnick/The Detroit News

Old for his age

Babcock broke into the NHL with Anaheim in 2002 and wasted little time building his own confidence. He took the Ducks within a game of winning the Cup Finals as a rookie coach, an unlikely run sparked by a first-round sweep of the top-seeded Wings.

But after missing the playoffs the following season, and spurred by front-office changes coming out of the 2004–05 lockout, Babcock bolted Anaheim for Detroit, where earlier this month he won his 200th career game. He's on pace to become the first NHL coach to win 50 or more games three consecutive seasons. And at 45, as he's occasionally reminded, he's actually 15 months younger than one of his players, Chelios.

"I may be young in this league, but I'm sure not a young coach," said Babcock, who got his first job coaching college hockey in Canada in 1987 and then worked his way up through the junior and minor pro ranks. "And yet I understand there's still huge room for growth."

And that, most everyone agrees, is Babcock's greatest strength.

"Mike wants to be the best coach in the world," said Ken Holland, general manager for the Red Wings. "He's committed, he's motivated, and he's all ears."

Jay Woodcroft, video coach for the Red Wings, calls Babcock "a visionary" when he's not busy scouring through countless hours of game footage looking for an edge. Almost daily, Babcock asks his assistants — Paul MacLean, Todd McLellan, and Woodcroft — the same question: "Are we as prepared as we can be?"

"Your preparation has to meet the size of the opportunity — that's his mantra," Woodcroft said. "And we've got a huge opportunity in front of us, so he wants to be as prepared as he can. You can see it in our play and our results: He never wants to be outworked."

Hard-working background

That work ethic was instilled in him at a young age, growing up in northern Manitoba and the Northwest Territories, "where there were 25 homes and a curling rink and it was 40-below all winter long," Babcock says, laughing.

His father, Mike Sr., was a mining engineer whose no-nonsense outlook forms the bedrock of his son's coaching philosophy: "He always told me 'You can never ask anyone to work harder than you're willing to work yourself.' So that's what we're trying to do."

"I read Bill Belichick's website every day," Babcock said, referring to the NFL coach whose Patriots played for their fourth Super Bowl title in seven years. "To me, he's the best coach in sports right now. He's got a machine there. And I think the Detroit Red Wings are the New England Patriots. That's how I want us to operate, from the top down."

That's a fair comparison, in many respects. The Wings' streak of 17 consecutive playoff appearances is the longest active run in U.S. major pro sports. And like the Patriots, they've managed to retool on the fly — winning three Cups with three different starting goaltenders in a six-year stretch, unearthing All-Stars like Pavel Datsyuk and Henrik Zetterberg in the later rounds of the draft, and remaining an elite team even after slashing their payroll in half coming out of the lockout.

But mostly they've cultivated a winning tradition

that even square-jawed Babcock didn't fully grasp as he prepared for his first camp in September 2005.

"He was interested to see how some of the veteran guys would react," said Kirk Maltby, a checking-line winger who has been with the team since 1996. "But I think, if anything, we surprised him with how hard we worked."

Added Holland: "I don't know how many times I said to him that first year, 'Mike, you don't get 100 points five consecutive years running a country club.' Our guys, if you give them a day off, they're not gonna go lounge by the pool all day. This is a highly motivated group.

"I think what he's learned to do over the time he's been here is he gives them more space today than he did three years ago. He has learned to respect them and they've learned to respect him."

Winning, of course, has a way of smoothing the rough patches. But in spite of the occasional grumbling, the players have responded well to his structured, up-tempo practices. ("It's been a good change: We needed someone new, something fresh," said Lidstrom, a 10-time All-Star.) And, slowly but surely, they've taken on some of Babcock's own characteristics.

"We play with more of an edge now," Holland said. "We're not gonna beat you up, but we don't back off, either. I think that's a credit to our players, but it's also a credit to Mike Babcock, who hammers that message to 'em every day."

Babcock is quick to point out he's a changed man, too.

"Our players have evolved, the game has evolved, I've evolved," Babcock said "It's not about ego, it's about winning. If you're willing to learn, you can learn a lot."

Said Holland: "A lot of things that Mike does sort of reminds me of Scotty, you know?"

Ace in the hole

That's hardly a coincidence. With a little help from Wings assistant GM Jim Nill, Babcock enlisted Scotty Bowman's help as an advisor after knocking off Detroit in the 2003 playoffs. And ever since Babcock joined the Wings, Bowman's role as a consultant has taken on a new twist — "almost like an assistant coach," Holland said.

"I knew he was the best coach in the world," Babcock said of Bowman, the winningest coach in NHL history. "But I didn't know the kind of man he is, and I never, ever knew we'd be friends. I'm not Scotty Bowman, and I don't pretend to be. But it's incredible to have that (opportunity). We talked yesterday, we'll talk today, we'll talk tomorrow."

Said Bowman: "He's got a lot of things going for him, but the thing that stands out to me is he's ultra-competitive. His train of thought was like mine: He's thinking about what he can do to get better all the time. He's intense, you know?"

So what has Babcock learned from his mentor?

"Sometimes talking too much doesn't do you any good," said Babcock, who lives in Northville with his wife, Maureen, and children Alexandra, Michael and Taylor. " 'When you don't talk,' Scotty always tells me, 'they don't know what you're thinking.'"

One thing Babcock has been thinking is how he'd love to get his name on the wall and get his hands on the Stanley Cup.

"Seen it, never touched it," Babcock said, nodding. "But I will one day."●

PLAYER BIOS
ANDREAS LILJA

No. 3, Defense
Height: 6-3, Weight: 228
Age: 32 (7-17-75)
Hometown: Helsin, Sweden
Comment: Replaced an injured
    Chelios late in playoffs and
    team didn't miss a beat.

	GP	G	A	Pts.	+/-	PIM
Season	79	2	10	12	-2	93
Playoffs	12	0	1	1	+3	16

PLAYER BIOS

NICKLAS LIDSTROM

No. 5, Defense
Height: 6-2, Weight: 185
Age: 38 (4-28-70)
Hometown: Vasteras, Sweden
Comment: Until being sidelined
    with a knee injury was
    getting attention as a
    MVP candidate.

	GP	G	A	Pts.	+/-	PIM
Season	76	10	60	70	+40	40
Playoffs	22	3	10	13	+8	14

PLAYER BIOS
DAN CLEARY

No. 11, Left Wing
Height: 6-1, Weight: 200
Age: 29 (12-18-78)
Hometown: Carbonear,
    Newfoundland
Comment: Made team as
    a tryout three seasons
    ago; earned a new
    five-year contract.

	GP	G	A	Pts.	+/-	PIM
Season	63	20	22	42	+21	33
Playoffs	22	2	1	3	+1	4

PLAYER BIOS
PAVEL DATSYUK

No. 13, Center
Height: 5-11, Weight: 180
Age: 29 (7-20-78)
Hometown: Sverdlovsk, Russia
Comment: Developed into one
    of NHL's premier two-way
    players.

	GP	G	A	Pts.	+/-	PIM
Season	82	31	66	97	+41	20
Playoffs	22	10	13	23	+13	6

PLAYER BIOS
DALLAS DRAKE

No. 17, Right Wing
Height: 6-1, Weight: 186
Age: 39 (2-4-69)
Hometown: Trail,
        British Columbia
Comment: Signed specifically
    for the playoffs and
    delivered when games
    mattered most.

	GP	G	A	Pts.	+/-	PIM
Season	65	3	3	6	-12	41
Playoffs	22	1	3	4	+2	12

PLAYER BIOS
KIRK MALTBY

No. 18, Right Wing
Height: 6-0, Weight: 193
Age: 35 (12-22-72)
Hometown: Guelph, Ontario
Comment: Still one of the best
    agitators in the league,
    mixing energy and
    defensive skills.

	GP	G	A	Pts.	+/-	PIM
Season	61	6	4	10	-8	32
Playoffs	12	0	1	1	E	10

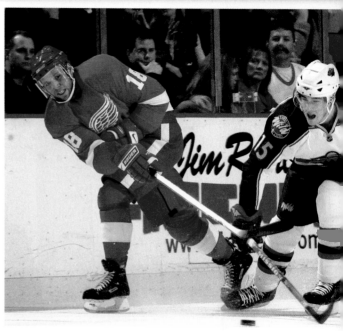

PLAYER BIOS
AARON DOWNEY

No. 20, Right Wing
Height: 6-1, Weight: 215
Age: 33 (8-27-74)
Hometown: Shelburne, Ontario
Comment: Quickly became fan
    favorite with willingness to
    stick up for teammates.

	GP	G	A	Pts.	+/-	PIM
Season	56	0	3	3	E	116
Playoffs	DNP					

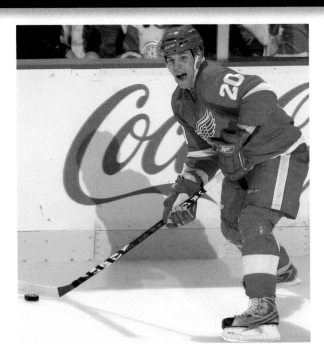

PLAYER BIOS
BRAD STUART

No. 23, Defense
Height: 6-2, Weight: 213
Age: 28 (11-6-79)
Hometown: Rocky Mountain
    House, Alberta
Comment: Acquired at trade
    deadline; provided
    physical, stay-at-home
    defense.

	GP	G	A	Pts.	+/-	PIM
Season	72	6	17	23	-10	69
Playoffs	21	1	6	7	+15	14

PLAYER BIOS
BRETT LEBDA

No. 22, Defense
Height: 5-11, Weight: 195
Age: 26 (1-15-82)
Hometown: Buffalo Grove,
 Illinois
Comment: Former undrafted
 free agent has become
 dependable, puck-moving
 defenseman.

	GP	G	A	Pts.	+/-	PIM
Season	78	3	11	14	-1	48
Playoffs	19	0	2	2	E	6

PLAYER BIOS
CHRIS CHELIOS

No. 24, Defense
Height: 6-0, Weight: 191
Age: 46 (1-25-62)
Hometown: Chicago, Illinois
Comment: At 46 he's earned
　　　　the respect of everyone
　　　　in the game.

	GP	G	A	Pts.	+/-	PIM
Season	69	3	9	12	+11	36
Playoffs	14	0	0	0	+2	10

PLAYER BIOS
DARREN McCARTY

No. 25, Forward
Height: 6-1, Weight: 210
Age: 36 (4-1-72)
Hometown: Burnaby,
        British Columbia
Comment: One of the all-time
        most popular Wings, his
        comeback was inspirational.

	GP	G	A	Pts.	+/-	PIM
Season	3	0	1	1	+2	0
Playoffs	17	1	1	2	+1	19

PLAYER BIOS
JIRI HUDLER

No. 26, Left Wing
Height: 5-10, Weight: 182
Age: 24 (1-4-84)
Hometown: Olomouc,
    Czech Republic
Comment: Quietly put
    together impressive
    playoff run after another
    steady regular season.

	GP	G	A	Pts.	+/-	PIM
Season	81	13	29	42	+11	26
Playoffs	22	5	9	14	-1	14

PLAYER BIOS
BRIAN RAFALSKI

No. 28, Defense
Height: 5-10, Weight: 191
Age: 34 (9-28-73)
Hometown: Dearborn, Michigan
Comment: A shrewd free-agent
   acquisition, his passing
   triggered the breakout.

	GP	G	A	Pts.	+/-	PIM
Season	73	13	42	55	+27	34
Playoffs	22	4	10	14	+6	12

PLAYER BIOS
CHRIS OSGOOD

No. 30, Goaltender
Height: 5-10, Weight: 178
Age: 35 (11-26-72)
Hometown: Peace River,
    Alberta
Comment: Started All-Star
    Game and carried team
    through the playoffs.

	GP	W	L	EGA	GAA	SV%
Season	43	27	9	4	2.09	.914
Playoffs	19	14	4	-	1.57	.930

PLAYER BIOS
KRIS DRAPER

No. 33, Center
Height: 5-10, Weight: 188
Age: 37 (5-24-71)
Hometown: Toronto, Ontario
Comment: Still one of the
best defensive forwards
in the league.

	GP	G	A	Pts.	+/-	PIM
Season	65	9	8	17	-2	68
Playoffs	22	3	1	4	E	10

PLAYER BIOS
MIKAEL SAMUELSSON

No. 37, Right Wing
Height: 6-2, Weight: 213
Age: 31 (12-23-76)
Hometown: Mariefred, Sweden
Comment: After disappointing
    regular season, came
    through with several big
    games in playoffs.

	GP	G	A	Pts.	+/-	PIM
Season	73	11	29	40	+21	26
Playoffs	22	5	8	13	+8	8

PLAYER BIOS
DOMINIK HASEK

No. 39, Goaltender
Height: 6-1, Weight: 166
Age: 43 (1-29-65)
Hometown: Pardubice,
    Czech Republic
Comment: At age 43, showed
    few signs of diminishing
    skills during regular season.

	GP	W	L	EGA	GAA	SV%
Season	41	27	20	3	2.14	.902
Playoffs	4	2	2	-	2.50	.888

PLAYER BIOS
HENRIK ZETTERBERG

No. 40, Center
Height: 5-11, Weight: 195
Age: 27 (10-9-80)
Hometown: Njurunda, Sweden
Comment: Like his buddy
    Datsyuk, he's become a
    complete player.

	GP	G	A	Pts.	+/-	PIM
Season	75	43	42	92	+30	34
Playoffs	22	13	14	27	+16	16

PLAYER BIOS
DARREN HELM

No. 43, Center
Height: 5-11, Weight: 172
Age: 21 (1-21-87)
Hometown: Winnipeg, Manitoba
Comment: Went from
    late-season promotion
    from minors to centering
    the fourth line in playoffs.

	GP	G	A	Pts.	+/-	PIM
Season	7	0	0	0	-2	2
Playoffs	18	2	2	4	+2	2

PLAYER BIOS

VALTTERI FILPPULA

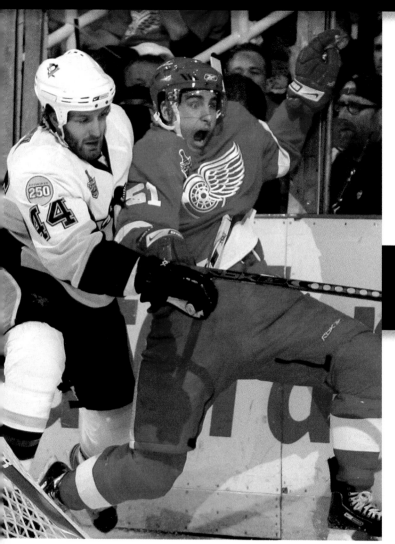

No. 51, Center
Height: 6-0, Weight: 193
Age: 24 (3-20-84)
Hometown: Vantaa, Finland
Comment: Took step toward
    developing into
    Zetterberg-Datsyuk-type
    two-way forward.

	GP	G	A	Pts.	+/-	PIM
Season	78	19	17	36	+16	28
Playoffs	22	5	6	11	+7	2

PLAYER BIOS
NIKLAS KRONWALL

No. 55, Defense
Height: 6-0, Weight: 189
Age: 27 (1-12-81)
Hometown: Stockholm, Sweden
Comment: Set a tone in playoffs
with bone-rattling hits.

	GP	G	A	Pts.	+/-	PIM
Season	65	7	28	35	+25	44
Playoffs	22	0	15	15	+16	18

PLAYER BIOS
JOHAN FRANZEN

No. 93, Left Wing
Height: 6-3, Weight: 220
Age: 28 (12-23-79)
Hometown: Vetlanda, Sweden
Comment: Amazing playoffs
    saw him break some of
    Gordie Howe's team marks.

	GP	G	A	Pts.	+/-	PIM
Season	72	27	11	38	+12	51
Playoffs	16	13	5	18	+13	14

PLAYER BIOS
TOMAS HOLMSTROM

No. 96, Right Wing
Height: 6-0, Weight: 200
Age: 35 (1-23-73)
Hometown: Pieta, Sweden
Comment: Injuries struck
    late in season, but was
    back causing havoc in
    playoffs.

	GP	G	A	Pts.	+/-	PIM
Season	59	20	20	40	+9	58
Playoffs	21	4	8	12	+4	26

OTHER CONTRIBUTORS

KYLE QUINCEY

No. 4, Defense • Height: 6-2, Weight: 207
Age: 22 (8-12-85) • Hometown: Kitchener, Ontario
Comment: A valued prospect; filled in admirably when injuries
hit in February.

	GP	G	A	Pts.	+/-	PIM
Season	6	0	0	0	-3	4

JUSTIN ABDELKADER

No. 8, Left wing • Height: 6-1, Weight: 215
Age: 21 (2-25-87) • Hometown: Muskegon, Michigan
Comment: Jumped in from Michigan State late in the season
and showed savvy and grit.

	GP	G	A	Pts.	+/-	PIM
Season	2	0	0	0	E	2

MATT ELLIS

No. 8, Left wing • Height: 6-0, Weight: 188
Age: 26 (8-31-81) • Hometown: Welland, Ontario
Comment: Released and claimed off waivers by L.A. Kings
in February.

	GP	G	A	Pts.	+/-	PIM
Season	35	2	4	6	+1	12

DEREK MEECH

No. 14, Defense • Height: 5-11, Weight: 182
Age: 24 (4-21-84) • Hometown: Winnipeg, Manitoba
Comment: Capitalized on opportunity when injuries stuck and
showed offensive skills.

	GP	G	A	Pts.	+/-	PIM
Season	32	0	3	3	-5	6

JIMMY HOWARD

No. 35, Goaltender • Height: 6-0, Weight: 205
Age: 24 (3-26-84) • Hometown: Syracuse, New York
Comment: Had an impressive season for Grand Rapids.

	GP	W	L	EGA	GAA	SV%
Season	4	0	2	0	2.13	.926

GARRETT STAFFORD

No. 36, Defense • Height: 6-0, Weight: 195
Age: 28 (1-28-80) • Hometown: Los Angeles, California
Comment: Filled in on defense when unit was decimated with
injuries in February.

	GP	G	A	Pts.	+/-	PIM
Season	2	0	0	0	E	0

MATTIAS RITOLA

No. 42, Center • Height: 6-0, Weight: 192
Age: 21 (3-14-87) • Hometown: Borlange, Sweden
Comment: Filled in briefly when forwards were hit
with injuries.

	GP	G	A	Pts.	+/-	PIM
Season	2	0	1	1	E	0

MARK HARTIGAN

No. 44, Center • Height: 6-0, Weight: 200
Age: 30 (10-15-77) • Hometown: Fort St. John, British
Columbia • Comment: Promoted late in season, gave fourth
line more offensive touch.

	GP	G	A	Pts.	+/-	PIM
Season	23	3	1	4	-2	16
Playoffs	4	0	1	1	E	4

TOMAS KOPECKY

No. 52, Defense • Height: 6-4, Weight: 206
Age: 24 (3-2-84) • Hometown: Karlskrona, Sweden
Comment: Last selection in 2002 draft, capable of becoming
a top-four caliber defenseman.

	GP	G	A	Pts.	+/-	PIM
Season	8	1	0	1	-3	4

By John Niyo

SUPERSCOUT
is Red Wings' European connection

Every good fishing guide has his secrets.

And it is no different with Hakan Andersson, the Wings' chief European scout who knows a thing or two about finding big fish in little ponds.

Before he began reeling in hockey players for the NHL's most successful franchise, Andersson was working as a charter guide for Fish & Game Frontiers. He'd lead tours in Norway in the summer, then head to Argentina in the winter. He'd spend the spring and fall on the water near his hometown of Stockholm, Sweden, guiding anglers in search of pike and salmon and sea trout.

These days, he's casting for a different kind of trophy catch. And mounted for display in these Stanley Cup Finals are nine European players that Andersson had a hand in signing or drafting. That list includes eight of the top 10 playoff scorers on the roster, only one of whom — defenseman Niklas Kronwall — was a first-round draft pick.

It's nothing new in Detroit, where the Wings were one of the first NHL teams to seriously scout hockey's heretofore hinterlands in Scandinavia and Russia. But luckily for the Wings, Christer Rockstrom, the scout who'd discovered Nick

Lidstrom, passed along Andersson's phone number when he left with Neil Smith to go to the New York Rangers in 1989.

Hidden gems

A decade later, Andersson convinced the Wings to draft Henrik Zetterberg in the seventh round, 210th overall. Pavel Datsyuk was a sixth-round selection, the 171st player drafted in 1998. Tomas Holmstrom went 257th in 1994. Valtteri Filppula was the 95th player taken in 2002. Throw in Johan Franzen, Jiri Hudler, and top prospects like Jonathan Ericsson — the very last pick of the 2002 draft — and it's easy to understand how the Wings have rebuilt on the fly while making the playoffs in 17 of Andersson's 18 seasons with the club.

"There's more and more people scouting Europe every year, so rarely does a player slip through the cracks anymore," Wings general manager Ken Holland said. "But you can still find the odd player who's off the radar screen."

Take Datsyuk, for instance. Nobody else would. Considered too small and slow, the shifty Russian center was passed over completely in two NHL

Hakan Andersson watches the Penguins and Red Wings practice before Game 3 of the Stanley Cup Finals. John T. Greilick/The Detroit News

drafts before Andersson, who noticed him while scouting another top junior player, decided the Wings should take a chance on him.

Zetterberg was deemed too small, too. But Andersson took note of his stats, kept an eye on him even after he'd been passed over for Sweden's world junior team, and "started investigating, wondering why they wouldn't pick him." He called former Wings first-round draft pick Anders Eriksson, whose brother played on Zetterberg's team, and he said, 'He's not a bad player.'

Later that winter, he showed Zetterberg to Wings assistant GM Jim Nill at a Swedish tournament. "And I said to him, 'That's a player that I want to draft.'" So they did, surprising even Zetterberg, who was vacationing with his parents when Andersson called with the good news.

"Part of being a good scout is what you see and your gut instinct," Holland said. "But it's also about information. And, obviously, Hakan's been in the business a long time now. He knows everybody. People trust him. They tell him things. So when he talks, we're going to listen."

Great approach

Anderson, who recently signed a two-year contract extension, is emboldened by the Wings' collegial approach.

"It's a great group, with no big egos," he said. "We all think, 'Well, my guy's got to be better than his guy.' But everybody's open-minded. And we look at players. We don't look at passports."

But Andersson also admits he's driven in part by fear.

"It'd be embarrassing," he says, if a Swedish prospect showed up unannounced on another team's roster.

There haven't been many that got away, but Andersson's still annoyed about losing one in the 2004 draft. Alexander Edler, a promising, 22-year-old defenseman for the Vancouver Canucks, was playing for a third-division pro team in Jamtland in the northern reaches of Sweden, up where the reindeer roam.

"And I was the only one person who knew about him as a prospect," Andersson said. "But then I made a crucial mistake."

The mistake he made was calling Edler's coach one day to say he was thinking of coming to watch a game. It was a seven-hour drive from Stockholm, so Andersson didn't want to waste the trip if Edler wasn't going to play that night.

But after he'd hung up, the coach called an agent, and the agent called a couple scouts. And as luck would have it, Vancouver's European scout, Thomas Gradin, made it to Jamtland for the final game of the season and saw Edler play. The Canucks then traded up to get a third-round selection in the 2004 draft — six spots ahead of Detroit — and drafted the Swede with the 91st overall pick.

"If I hadn't made that call, we would've had him," Andersson said. "I could have found out another way if he was going to play or not. It was a stupid mistake."

Of course, six picks after Edler, the Wings drafted another player on Andersson's wish list: Johan Franzen.

"But we could've got him in the fourth round," he said. "We could've had them both. That still bugs me." ●

Fans congratulate Pavel Datsyuk as he walks off the ice at the end of Game 6 in Nashville.
David Guralnick/The Detroit News

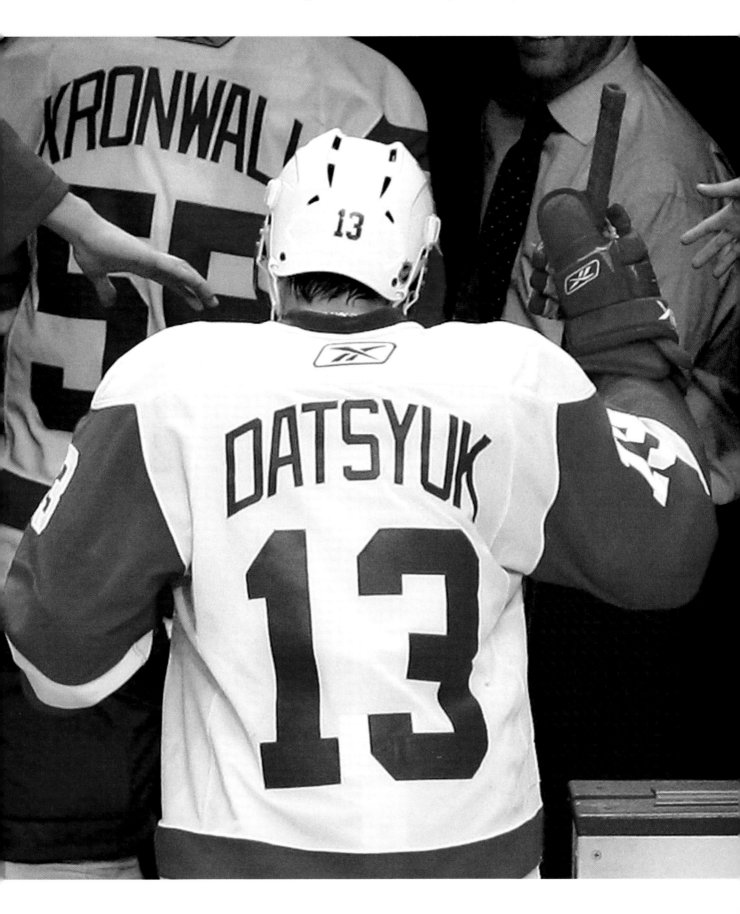

By John Niyo

FRANZEN

Stubborn as a mule

Equinely speaking, the Wings' Johan Franzen remains a work in progress.

Team captain and fellow countryman Nick Lidstrom, when asked to describe Franzen's greatest asset as a hockey player, quickly drew a picture of a donkey. Figuratively, at least.

"His stubbornness," Lidstrom answered, laughing.

Moments later, teammate Niklas Kronwall, another Swede, offered a different description: "Right now, he's a horse for us."

Actually, he's the Wings' "Mule" — a nickname Steve Yzerman branded him with during his first training camp in Traverse City back in 2005.

"At first, I don't think he really knew what it meant. He didn't know if it was a good thing or a bad thing," Kronwall said of Franzen. "But now I think he's proud of it."

Given a chance to play a bigger part offensively for the Wings due to a rash of injuries this winter, Franzen, 28, in his third NHL season, has stubbornly refused to retreat to a supporting role.

But while his game has changed, said Lidstrom, "That nickname's going to stick with him, he's got no choice."

That's fine with the Mule — or "Mula," in Swedish.

"It's easy to remember, at least," joked Franzen, who's hardly the quarreling type, though at 6'3" and 220 pounds, he's beginning to learn how to throw his weight around on the ice.

Off it, he's still largely a pushover, whether it's watching movies at home with his girlfriend of seven years, Cecilia, or lounging around the team hotel.

"He likes to take it easy," said Kronwall, Franzen's roommate on the road. "He sleeps a lot. But other than that, he's pretty normal."

And while neither player fits the stereotypical Swedish mold — Kronwall's lethal open-ice hitting drew plenty of attention during the playoffs — things remain blissfully neutral away from the rink. No fights over the remote control, and only minor grumbling about viewing preferences.

"He likes to watch his nature shows," Kronwall said, "and I'm more into the reality TV."

Even the late-night phone calls are kept to a minimum.

"I'm not much for talking on the phone," said Franzen, who still spends his summers near his hometown of Vetlanda in southern Sweden. "I

Johan Franzen tries to get the puck past Nashville goaltender Dan Ellis in the first period.
David Guralnick/The Detroit News

don't want to hear people back home being too positive. I don't want to hear that. There's a long way to go. You don't want to start ..."

And then he interrupted himself, throwing his right arm over his shoulder and patting himself on the back.

"That's the good thing — he's never gonna change," Kronwall said. "No matter what happens, he always remembers where he came from."

But where did he come from? That's a question NHL teams often find themselves asking when it comes to the Wings' roster.

Sure, five of the team's top six forwards are homegrown draft picks, but their average draft position was 166th overall.

General manager Ken Holland actually selected Franzen sight unseen in the third round (97th overall) of the 2004 entry draft. Hakan Andersson, the Wings' chief European scout, liked the size and skill level he saw in Franzen, a late-bloomer who "figured I was too old" to get a shot at the NHL. A breakout 2003–04 season in the Swedish Elite League changed that, and after the lockout, Franzen, who'd spent a couple summers working factory jobs, finally got a chance to make a name for himself.

First, though, he had to shake a few old habits.

"I remember the first time I saw him, he was a big guy who could skate, but all he thought about was defense," Holland said. "I thought there was more offense in his game."

There was, obviously. But this much? Few could've predicted the record-setting pace Franzen set this spring. He scored 14 goals in the month of March alone, and broke Gordie Howe's franchise record with six game-winners among them.

Henrik Zetterberg and Pavel Datsyuk still draw most of the attention, "but he's the next guy you've gotta worry about," Colorado coach Joel Quenneville said.

Added Avs defenseman John-Michael Liles: "He's got that frame and that build to be a prototypical power forward. And he's starting to really live up to that, toward the end of the season and here in the playoffs. He's somebody that you've got to be aware of. He's a dangerous player, for sure."

A player Holland aims to keep, too, by the way. Franzen is signed through next season at a cap-friendly salary number of just under $950,000. But beginning July 1, the Wings can sign him — as well as Zetterberg — to an extension.

"Between the end of the season and training camp, I'd like to have some conversations with Johan (and his agent)," Holland said Friday. "Obviously, we want to keep him here. And I'm sure he likes it here.... So now we have to find a number that works for both of us."

That number keeps climbing as Franzen keeps scoring, no doubt. So does the Mule's profile.

"He's kind of a quiet guy and he says he doesn't want to be in the spotlight too much," Lidstrom said. "But the way he's playing, he's going to be there." ●

Johan Franzen celebrates his second-period goal against Nashville's Chris Mason. It was Franzen's second goal of the game. David Guralnick/The Detroit News

By John Niyo

BRAT PACK
Red Wings' class of '93 now team leaders

They drive to work now, which is a sign they're no longer the kids they were in those team photos, the ones that hang like pages from a high school yearbook in the hallway outside the Red Wings dressing room at Joe Louis Arena.

And come to think of it, they even drive their kids to school now, which makes this mini-reunion tour for the Brat Pack — the Wings' rookie class of 1993 — all the more nostalgic.

Nearly 15 years after they began their NHL careers together in Detroit, Kris Draper, Chris Osgood, and Darren McCarty can't help but wonder where the time has gone, even as they marvel — on the eve of the 2008 Stanley Cup playoffs — at the memories they're still sharing.

"I just remember sitting around back in those first few years and saying, 'Holy (expletive), look at how old these guys are,'" McCarty said, laughing for old time's sake. "Guys like Stevie (Yzerman), they were maybe 30-31 is all, but we were like, 'Man, they're so old.' Now, I'm sitting here at 36 saying, 'I'm not that old, am I? I don't feel 36.'

"But the young guys are probably saying the same thing about us."

Probably so. But chances are, they won't be saying the same thing McCarty is today 15 years from now.

"The day I walked in this dressing room, I just kind of thought, 'Take it all in — you don't know how long it's going to last,'" Drapper said. "And to sit here, 15 years later, having been a part of the success we've had and the Stanley Cups we've won, it's unbelievable. I'm proud to be able to say that it has lasted this long."

And it does seem like "forever ago," as Osgood put it, that he and Darren McCarty were 20-year-olds sharing a roof in upstate New York — minor-league hockey players with major-league dreams.

"I lived upstairs, he lived downstairs," said McCarty, Detroit's second-round pick in the 1992 NHL entry draft who, like Osgood, played one full season with the AHL's Adirondack Red Wings. "And all we did was play the '93 Sega hockey game. We'd take those big Gatorade containers and we'd spit sunflower seeds into 'em, and then we'd tape 'em up and it'd be like the Stanley Cup. I was always Chicago, Ozzie was Vancouver."

Soon, though, they'd be playing for real. McCarty, a rugged right wing who racked up 278

Teammates congratulate Darren McCarty after he scored in the first period, his first goal since returning to the NHL. David Guralnick/The Detroit News

penalty minutes with Adirondack in 1992–93, fought his way onto the Wings' roster in training camp. Osgood, a third-round draft pick in 1991, made the team as Tim Cheveldae's backup and "ended up playing way more than I ever imagined." Draper, who'd been acquired the summer before from Winnipeg for the princely sum of $1, got called up from Adirondack at midseason.

"I was nervous, excited — you know, the whole deal," said Draper, who'll turn 37 next month. "Ozzie and Mac were already here, and so was Marty Lapointe. I remember when I got in here and saw my locker — 'Draper 33' — it was right next to Ozzie's and I thought, 'Oh, good: One of the younger guys.' But back then, Ozzie was painfully quiet."

A friendship is born

So much so, in fact, that the two barely spoke a word for more than a week despite being locker-room neighbors.

"Then one day — I think he'd gone out the night before — I finally turned to him and said 'What'd you do last night?'" Osgood, 36, remembers. "He just answered, 'You wanna go out tonight?' That's how it started."

"And from there," adds Draper, "we just became best friends — we did everything together."

A few weeks later, after getting word from then-general manager Bryan Murray that he'd be sticking around, Draper packed up his bags, checked out of the Ponchartrain Hotel and moved in with Osgood in Farmington Hills. The next year, they moved back downtown to the Riverfront Apartments, separated from their office by an empty parking lot and a couple chain link fences.

"Sometimes we drove to practice, but other times we'd walk and we'd just hop the fences," Osgood said. "We'd get up at 11:30 in the morning and just cruise over."

They'd leave behind half-eaten casseroles in the microwave, empty beer cans on the table, maybe even a stray, straggling teammate on the couch. And if the whole arrangement had the feel of a college fraternity house, it was for good reason. The Wings were the hottest ticket in town, and this band of Canadian-born brothers — McCarty, Draper, Osgood, Lapointe, and occasionally Kirk Maltby, who joined the team in 1996 — was the life of the party, in many respects.

"We were all just living out our dreams, you know?" Draper said. "We were playing for the best organization in hockey, we were winning a lot of games and it was just fun to be a part of it all. I remember thinking back then: 'I never want this to end.' I wanted every day to be Groundhog Day."

For years, it was, though that also meant things never ended well. And while the kids didn't bear the same scars the veterans on that team did — players like Yzerman and Dino Ciccarelli and Shawn Burr — they quickly accumulated their own brief history of playoff disappointments. A first-round loss to San Jose in 1994 that left Osgood in tears, getting swept by New Jersey in the Cup finals in 1995, and then the record-setting 1995–96 season that ended with a loss in Colorado and Draper hospitalized with severe facial injuries, courtesy of Claude Lemieux.

"For us, I think the big thing was losing in '95," McCarty said. "I remember standing by the net

Kris Draper, left, and Brett Lebda celebrate after a goal against the Calgary Flames in Joe Louis Arena. David Guralnick/The Detroit News

with Drapes watching (the Devils) celebrate and him saying, 'That's gonna be us.' But we didn't really realize how hard it was gonna be until we lost the next year and it was like '(Expletive), we may never get back there again.' That was our biggest lesson, I think."

Learning, growing

There would be other lessons learned, of course. And more failures, too, most notably the ones that McCarty's still making amends for, after years of battling alcohol and substance abuse.

"We were all growing as hockey players, but we were all growing as people, too," Draper said. "And we all went through it together, which is what made winning that Cup in '97 so special."

That they played significant roles in that championship run — and the ones that would follow — made it even more so. McCarty, who'd made his first trip to rehab the summer before, soon replaced Joe Kocur on the "Grind Line" with Draper and Maltby, and they knew their role as an in-your-face checking unit was their meal ticket.

"We were the motor," McCarty said. "We were the parts inside the machine — the heartbeat, the pulse."

Still, things started to change after the first Cup victory. Girlfriends became wives, bachelors became fathers.

"We'd still hang out at the rink and have our laughs, but instead of going home to Ozzie, I was going home to Julie, which wasn't a bad thing," laughed Draper, who married his wife in 1998.

Draper now is married with three children. Osgood and his wife, Jenna, a Michigan native, have two daughters. McCarty, meanwhile, is busy reconnecting with his ex-wife Cheryl and their four kids after spending the last two years in Calgary.

Things were different at the rink, too.

"We never brought it up with each other, but I know we all thought it," Draper said. "As we were getting older we were also taking on more responsibilities with the team, getting bigger roles. But we all thought, 'Well, if we keep winning, they're not gonna break us up.'"

Eventually, they would. Lapointe left in July 2001, signing a big free-agent contract with Boston. Osgood was sent packing a few months later after the Wings traded for goalie Dominik Hasek, a two-time MVP.

"But as disappointed as I was to see Ozzie leave," Draper said, "I was just as excited when he gave me that call to say he was coming back (after the 2004–05 NHL lockout)."

Ditto the heart-to-heart talk he had last fall with McCarty, whose contract was bought out by Detroit after the lockout. McCarty was out of the league this season until Draper helped him get a minor-league tryout with the Flint Generals, a team he co-owns. Three months later, here he is, back on the Wings playoff roster and feeling like a kid again, just hoping for a chance to contribute. And, yes, he and Osgood are still playing video games — only now it's Xbox 360 online.

"For me to have the opportunity to come back, when you look at the big picture, it's just the way it's supposed to be," McCarty said, a bit wistfully.

On that count, he'll get no argument from his pals.

"You don't really appreciate it until you get to where we are now, how special it was for us to play for this long together," said Osgood, who signed a contract extension in January that'll keep him in Detroit through 2010–11, just like Draper. "We all started out together, and we'd like to finish together — that'd be pretty cool." ●

Chris Osgood stops a shot by the Penguins in the first game of the Stanley Cup Finals at Joe Louis Arena. Dale G. Young/The Detroit News

By Robert Snell and Mike Wilkinson

HOMETOWN
Wings turn Novi into 'Little Sweeden'

So one day there's a stack of wood and jungle gym equipment piled on Detroit Red Wings defenseman Andreas Lilja's lawn.

Neighbor Gene Bigi recalls that another neighbor offered to help build the play set.

"No, I'll have some of my friends come over," Lilja replied.

The "friends" turned out to be fellow Swedes on the Detroit Red Wings. In Metro Detroit, six of the team's seven Swedish players live within five miles of each other in Novi, prompting coach Mike Babcock to recently dub the suburb "Little Sweden."

The concentration is no accident. It gives the foreign-born players comfort to live near each other where they can speak Swedish and where their wives, girlfriends and kids can socialize during the team's long and frequent road trips.

"For me, I picked Novi because my wife wanted to live close to some countrymen," winger Mikael Samuelsson said. "You've got to have a convenient situation for the family and it helps the guys here too. It helps me relax when I'm on the road. I know they're having a good time."

In pockets, Novi is so saturated with Swedish

Wings that certain neighborhoods look like the team's locker room. Lilja lives in a red (naturally) brick house across the street from Samuelsson, his carpool pal. Both live a few subdivisions away from Niklas Kronwall, who is south of Johan Franzen's house, which is a block away from Valtteri Filppula's place. He's Finnish, but as a fellow Scandinavian, it is close enough.

Captain Nicklas Lidstrom lives a few miles southwest.

Teammate Tomas Holmstrom loves Novi so much he bought a new home last month nine houses away from his old one.

The only Swedish holdout: star forward Henrik Zetterberg, who lives in Bloomfield Hills.

"They've got like their own city within the city," joked teammate Kirk Maltby, a former Novi resident. "They've got their IKEA out there somewhere."

Indeed, Novi offers a direct 15-minute drive along I-275 to the Swedish home-furnishings mega-store in Canton.

"Perfect distance," Kronwall said.

The Novi trend apparently started with Lidstrom, the team's captain, who has been a Red Wing since 1991.

And like other immigrants, such as the many

Andreas Lilja, Kris Draper, Henrik Zetterberg, and Brett Lebda celebrate Draper's goal in the second period. David Guralnick/The Detroit News

Japanese who have chosen Novi, the Swedes who followed Lidstrom picked Novi.

Mayor David Landry, who recently honored Lidstrom for his work with the local youth hockey program, said the Swedes are in Novi for the same reason the city has a sizeable Japanese population: It has good schools and welcoming residents.

"We respect their privacy and we're happy that they're here," he said.

In 2000, the census estimated there were 840 people of Swedish ancestry in Novi, less than 2 percent of the city's population. A number of other Oakland County communities, such as Milford Township, Royal Oak and Bloomfield Township, had higher concentrations of Swedes.

Kronwall bought his Novi home last year and said the number of Swedish teammates in that city helped convince him to buy, but it wasn't the only reason.

"I just really liked the area. It's a bit more family-oriented," he said. "More calm. The people in general are really nice."

The team's playoff success — they are two wins from a Stanley Cup championship — is generating excitement among neighbors. A Red Wings jersey hangs on the front door of a home near Holmstrom's house, while a neighbor two doors down from Samuelsson scrawled "Go Wings" on the driveway in chalk alongside a hand-sketched Stanley Cup.

Lilja neighbor Krystn Masnari first met Samuelsson last spring when the Red Wing stopped by to introduce himself.

"He was very humble. He said, 'I'm not sure if you've met my friend Andreas, we work together,'" Masnari recalled Samuelsson saying. 'We play for a team you might have heard of. It's called the Red Wings.'

"I said, 'Yeah, I've heard of it.' "

But celebrity brings temptation.

Last winter, Samuelsson built a snowman. Instead of a corncob pipe, button nose and broomstick, he made it with memorabilia, one of his own hockey sticks.

Masnari's son Jonathan, a huge hockey fan, craved the stick.

"I said 'Jonathan, you cannot go swipe that hockey stick. Leave it alone,'" Masnari said.

Playoff excitement is more difficult to bottle.

"We have been excited for a while, but we're trying not to make them feel uncomfortable with it," she said.

Bigi, who also lives nearby, said the Wings are nice, unassuming neighbors, so other residents return the favor.

"We don't bother them, we just say 'Hi' if we see them on the street," Bigi said. "If they've got time, neighbors will talk to them. But not something like 'Hey, can you get us tickets?'"

Urban Lundberg, a local businessman and president of the Swedish American Chamber of Commerce of Detroit, said all Swedes get an unintended yet welcome boost from the team's — and its Swedish players' — success.

"When the Red Wings are doing well, the quality of Swedish goods is higher," Lundberg chuckled. ●

Detroit's Tomas Holmstrom, left, and Henrik Zetterberg chat on the bench.
David Guralnick/The Detroit News

By Vartan Kupelian

LIDSTROM'S LEGEND
Performance invites comparisons to Orr

The images are indelible. Number 4 is carrying the puck, hapless pursuers in his wake. He's skating circles to kill penalties.

He's stickhandling and shooting.

Finally, he's soaring through the air and scoring another goal for the ages.

Bobby Orr played defense like nobody else ever has. He played with flair and passion, pure instinct and brilliance.

Today, Orr watches the NHL, the league he dominated for a decade between 1966 and 1976, from a unique perspective.

He knows what's good and what's not, especially when the subject is how to play defense.

That means Orr can appreciate like few others just how good Nicklas Lidstrom has been for a very long time.

"I've watched him a lot," Orr said. "He does everything."

That's Robert Gordon Orr, the greatest defenseman ever, speaking.

"Lidstrom is a guy who comes every night."

"His performance is the same every game. He's as consistent a player as I've seen."

"He's got great passion. There has never been a great player who didn't have great passion or great vision."

Best of his generation

Nobody will suggest Lidstrom, the Wings' peerless defenseman, is Bobby Orr. What they are likely to argue is that there hasn't been anybody better than Lidstrom at the position over the past 16 seasons and maybe even since Orr left the NHL in 1979.

In his prime, Orr won every possible honor. Twice, in 1969–70 and 1974–75, he became the only defenseman to win the scoring title.

He won the Hart Trophy as Most Valuable Player three times and twice was the playoff MVP for leading the Boston Bruins to the Stanley Cup in 1970 and 1972.

In 1970, Orr was *Sports Illustrated's* Man of the Year, a rare honor for a hockey player.

The Norris Trophy as the league's best defenseman was Orr's birthright. He won it eight straight years beginning in 1968.

It is a mark approached by very few. Doug Harvey, who played for Montreal and the New York Rangers, won the Norris Trophy seven times

Nicklas Lidstrom, who became the first new Red Wings captain in more than two decades, is blocked by Stars forward Jere Lehtinen in the third period. David Guralnick/The Detroit News

offense and produce points in bunches. It was always difficult, if not quite impossible, for opponents to play offense when Orr was on the ice.

They were all too busy trying to prevent Orr from beating them with his offense. That was an innovative approach to defense.

In perhaps the highest compliment Lidstrom has ever received, Orr said he sees "some similarities" in their games.

"He does the things I like to see a defenseman do," Orr said. "He reads the ice — all the great players read the ice — and he does it as well as anybody. There haven't been many like him when it comes to reading what's happening. He sees what's going to happen.

"The way he shoots the puck, passes, anticipates, jumps up — or doesn't jump up — he does everything."

Understanding the game

The feel for a game is innate.

Instincts aren't taught, they're the product of an intuitive understanding of how a game is played and are nurtured over a period of time. Lidstrom arrived in Detroit as an offensive defenseman and power-play specialist. With experience and a solid work ethic, he has matured into a five-time Norris Trophy winner.

The vision, Lidstrom said: "You just have it.

before Orr. Raymond Bourque won it five times as Orr's successor with the Bruins.

And now Lidstrom has won it five times since the 2000–2001 season. In 2003, Lidstrom became the first defenseman since Orr to win the Norris Trophy three straight years. Another for Lidstrom this year is a distinct likelihood.

Orr is considered one of the three greatest players in hockey history alongside Gordie Howe and Wayne Gretzky. Each defined his position. It wasn't until after Howe that the term "power forward" was identified. Gretzky combined sublime playmaking skills — the calling card of any great center — with scoring skills never before displayed even by the purest snipers.

Orr demonstrated that defensemen could also play

(above) Johan Franzen, left, and Nicklas Lidstrom sit for a group photo amongst the volunteers (and their families) that helped out at Centre Ice Arena during training camp.
David Guralnick/The Detroit News

(opposite) Jesse and Marty Jenter of Novi climb the steps to hockey heaven as the Red Wings host the Penguins in the first game of the Stanley Cup Finals at Joe Louis Arena.
Dale G. Young/The Detroit News

"I played other sports growing up and developed that sense," he said. "As the years have gone by, I've adjusted to playing in the NHL and worked hard (on it).

"The game is so fast, you have to have instincts. You don't have time to think about much. I've been able to develop that."

For all the things he does, Lidstrom is the mainspring for the Wings. He is their Bobby Orr, minus the flash and dash. For all these years, Lidstrom has played defense like Jean Beliveau played center for those superlative Montreal teams — with elegance and grace.

"It's everything he does," said Johan Franzen, Lidstrom's Swedish teammate with the Wings.

"All his numbers speak for themselves. He's so calm. He's always buying himself time. He never seems to be under pressure somehow."

Lidstrom, who was born in 1970, never saw Orr play, live or on television. Lidstrom has seen highlight reels and he learned of Orr's reputation from teammates.

"When I first came to Detroit, the older defensemen on the team, like Paul Coffey and Brad McCrimmon, would talk about Orr," said Lidstrom, whose idol growing up was another defenseman from Sweden, Borje Salming.

A year ago *The Hockey News* called Lidstrom the best European-born player ever in the NHL.

Follow the leader

The Wings' defense feeds off its leader. It's a group known for its mobility and savvy. Its strength is in the ability to move the puck and get it out of the defensive end with as little fuss as possible, just

the way coaches appreciate.

It's a defense that anticipates the play and attacks when the opportunity arises.

The Wings' defenders aren't especially big or physical. A bump-and-grind style isn't what they do best.

Now consider Lidstrom's style. He's mobile and savvy. His strength is the ability to move the puck, get it out of the defensive end with as little fuss as possible.

He's a player who anticipates the play and attacks.

At 6'1", 193 pounds, Lidstrom is big enough but not physical. He doesn't bump and grind. It's not in his makeup or his game.

The similarities are not a coincidence.

"If the other defensemen on the team aren't watching him, they should be ashamed of themselves," Orr said. "I know if I'm playing with Lidstrom, I'd be watching him."

Lidstrom is the conductor. He plays 20 minutes or more a game and pulls the strings on the power play. He orchestrates the tempo, dictates the style and the others follow. "That's exactly as it should be," Orr said.

"Knowing the big guy is there, it contributes at both ends," Orr said. "It's a pretty warm feeling.

"With young players, it disturbs me a little bit when I hear coaches say, 'Don't carry it, shoot it up.' What makes our game so great is the ability to do things like carrying it out and making plays. That's how we find the Paul Coffeys and Nicklas Lidstroms.

"I enjoyed the game so much playing that way. I don't think I could play it any other way."

And today Orr couldn't enjoy watching it nearly as much without Nicklas Lidstrom playing defense the way he does. ●

Fans try to get the attention of Nicklas Lidstrom during warmups before a game against the Predators at Joe Louis Arena. David Guralnick/The Detroit News

By John Niyo

SEEING CLEARY
Faulkner paves way for fellow Newfoundlanders

Alex Faulkner was on the phone, his voice crackling over the line from his home in Bishop's Falls, Newfoundland. He was reading the morning paper and reminiscing as the cover of the St. John's Evening Telegraph carried a photograph of a young Faulkner in a Detroit Red Wings uniform, scoring a goal against Johnny Bower and Tim Horton and the Toronto Maple Leafs some 45 years ago.

"Sometimes, I say to my wife, 'It almost doesn't seem real,' " said Faulkner, 72, who played two seasons (1962–64) alongside Gordie Howe & Co. "It wasn't a long time. It was a great time for a short time. But, boy, I'll tell ya, even now I guess it's the small-town boy in me it's almost too much for me to even fathom that I really was there."

"But then," he adds, chuckling, "here's the picture."

And here's the reason: Up until now, Faulkner was the first Newfoundlander ever to play in the NHL, and the only one ever to play in the Stanley Cup Finals, something he did twice in his brief career. But along came the 2007–08 Red Wings and Dan Cleary or "Danny," as his fellow Newfies call him and suddenly Faulkner's phone is ringing a little more often than usual.

"He's revived all the memories, I'll tell you that," Faulkner said, laughing. "So I thank him for that."

Spreading their wings

Cleary, of course, offers thanks in return. A native of tiny Riverhead, Newfoundland, he actually was born 10 minutes down the road in Carbonear "because that's where the hospital is." And Cleary, 29, grew up playing hockey in nearby Harbour Grace, the same fishing port where Faulkner's senior career started, even though Bishop's Falls is a four-hour drive west. Both NHLers played for the Conception Bay CeeBees before leaving home to try to make it as pros.

"He's like the pioneer of Newfoundland hockey, really," Cleary said. "Nobody was coming from Newfoundland to play in the NHL. So he kind of paved the way.

That's no small chore, either. It's a hard road to prosperity coming from "The Rock," as the locals affectionately call this remote Canadian Atlantic province, owing to its rugged coastline and largely uninhabitable interior. Visitors here or "come-from-aways" are treated to a "Screech-In" welcome,

Detroit's Daniel Cleary and Edmonton's Steve Staios fight for the puck in the first period.
David Guralnick/The Detroit News

which consists of a diabolical rum-like liquor ("screech") and a smooch with a dead fish. Those who are born on The Rock tend to die there, too.

For hockey players, it's not much different, with the lack of exposure to top-tier competition or pro scouts. Cleary is one of three current Newfoundland-born NHLers along with San Jose's Ryane Clowe and Montreal's Michael Ryder.

"If you don't leave, you won't go anywhere in hockey, so I'm glad I left when I did," said Cleary, who rattles off a few names of players, including local legend Andy Sullivan, who had the talent but never got away.

Cleary left at age 14 to play junior hockey in Kingston, Ontario. He later starred for the Belleville Bulls in the Ontario Hockey League and was a top-15 NHL draft pick in 1997. Still, with a lackluster work ethic and a wayward off-ice life earlier in his career, Cleary, now happily married with a 2-year-old daughter, needed the better part of a decade before he found a stable home in Detroit with his fourth NHL team.

Lifetime of memories

Faulkner hasn't seen Cleary play in person, "but I've been following him for years." Likewise, Cleary's never met Faulkner, though Cleary's father, Kevin, used to watch him play.

"But Alex Faulkner was certainly someone I knew of growing up," Dan Cleary said. "I mean, imagine how talented you'd have to be to play in the Original Six?"

Faulkner centered a line with Bruce MacGregor and Larry Jeffrey when the Wings advanced to back-to-back Finals. He scored five goals — three

game-winners — in eight playoff games in 1963, before a hand injury effectively ended his career the following season.

Still, he laughs as he recalls his historic NHL debut in December 1961. He played one game that season for Toronto at the old Montreal Forum.

"That morning, I had two soft-boiled eggs for breakfast and I couldn't eat them," he said. "I couldn't swallow, I was so nervous. After that, it got easier. Thank goodness for that."

Faulkner has stayed up late watching the Wings' games — Newfoundland Daylight Time actually is 90 minutes ahead of the Eastern time zone — even though his days are busy with running a senior citizens' center and an RV park. And while much of the Maritimes were cheering for Pittsburgh — the Penguins' Sidney Crosby hails from Nova Scotia — Faulkner was cheering for the home team.

"It's exciting to all of us, being Newfoundlanders," he said. "We're very much, I guess you'd say, 'Rock' people. We really do back each other up, and we just love where we live. This place has got a lot of negatives, like bad weather most of the time, but we're very loyal to each other."

So what would happen if Cleary brought the Cup home with him this summer?

"I have thought about it, yeah," Cleary said. "I honestly don't know what to expect, but it's certainly something that I burn for, you know? I want it so bad. Not only for that reason, obviously. But it would be so cool to be the first Newfoundlander to have their name on the Cup, and to be able to bring it home and share it with everybody."

"And, you know, I just think we're due," he added with a smile. "We're due." ●

Daniel Cleary warms up before a game against the Colorado Avalanche at Joe Louis Arena.
David Guralnick/The Detroit News

By Bob Wojnowski

KRONWALL OF PAIN
Defenseman makes heavy impact with physical play

Usually, they don't even see him coming. They'll be skating along, head down, chasing the puck, and then there he is, all arms and legs and fuzzy beard, clobbering the player right into a video highlight.

For the longest time, we didn't see him coming either. Niklas Kronwall was half-myth and half-misfortune, a heavy-hitting defenseman who always seemed to suffer the flukiest injuries, knocking him out of the playoffs, damaging the Red Wings' chances more than we ever knew.

Now we know. Fully healthy, Kronwall is becoming the Wall of Kron, adding nasty bite to the Wings' smooth-skating attack. Surely you've seen the latest highlight of an open-ice blasting.

Kronwall skates on the finest edge, the one not many players dare straddle. Coach Mike Babcock calls him a "predator" because he hunts for the hit that does more than separate a player from the precious puck.

It sets a rollicking tone. Or sends a stern message. Or rattles a tooth.

"Any time a team comes into your building, you want them to know it's gonna be tough to beat you," Kronwall said. "I've always enjoyed the physi-

cal part of the game. It gets the adrenaline rushing a little bit. After that one (on Miettinen), it took a couple minutes to settle down and go back to work."

These Wings can rile up quickly and proved it in last year's playoffs, when they matched physical opponents and reached the conference final. With Kronwall and newcomer Brad Stuart banging gleefully, and Babcock pushing for more, the Wings still don't play nice nearly as often.

Brutal artwork

But let's not make this into something it's not. The Wings aren't bruisers and Kronwall isn't a head-hunter, or even a headline-hunter. He's a smart, low-key guy who's becoming a difference-maker, and who views the open-ice hit as something of an art, an art we haven't seen regularly around here since the great Vladimir Konstantinov a decade ago.

Foes may fume but teammates marvel at the ability to line up a player in wide-open spaces and send him flying, without using a dirty elbow or an unnecessary leap.

"I don't have any clue how Nik does it," Chris Chelios said. "I've tried it and end up with my eyes

Detroit's Niklas Kronwall is chased by former teammate Robert Lang of the Blackhawks.
David Guralnick/The Detroit News

closed and missing everything. I'm more of a hitting-around-the-boards guy. It's all timing. Some guys have that gift and he's obviously one of the best. This is what everybody was hoping he'd turn into."

It must be timing because it can't be size. Kronwall is 6', 189 pounds, not counting the weight of his beard.

"In the past, I've rushed things and tried to take too many risks out there," Kronwall, 27, said. "Now, playing a whole season, I feel more comfortable. When there's a chance to step up, do it. When it's not there, stay home."

Then he added with a smile: "So far, so good."

Sorry, but you have to add it. On a starry team, Kronwall has been horribly star-crossed, appearing in just six playoff games in three previous seasons because of mostly fluky injuries.

In January 2004, he broke a leg when he stepped in a rut in the ice during pregame warmups in Los Angeles and was out for the season.

In 2005, he missed the first 52 games because of a torn ligament in his left knee.

Last season, he missed 14 games because of a groin injury, then late in March suffered a fractured sacrum (tailbone area) on a relatively tame check and was lost for the playoffs.

This season, he missed four games because of a groin injury and 13 because of a shoulder injury but — knock on fiberglass — played in 65 games and ranked fifth among NHL defensemen in plus-minus (plus 25).

Naturally, he's not a big fan of revisiting the past.

Only one way to play

"Did I ever curse my luck?" he said. "No, I try not to think about it. I know I can't change my style just because I've had some freak injuries. I only know how to play one way. I still have a lot to work on, but there's nothing that would keep me from throwing my body around."

Kronwall says it matter-of-factly, not boastfully. His unpleasant on-ice style doesn't mesh with his pleasant off-ice demeanor. It's one of the weird dichotomies in sports — the toughest competitors often are the most mild-mannered people.

"He is a relatively quiet, calm guy," teammate Kirk Maltby said. "He doesn't want to hurt a guy or take his head off. He's just very strong on his skates, deceivingly strong. When he catches a guy looking for a puck, by the time he turns around, it's too late."

But while opponents sometimes mutter, there are very few accusations of cheap shots.

"He's an intelligent, intelligent player," Babcock said. "He sees when a guy is vulnerable and he's got that ability to hunt you down. It's important that he and Stuart are always on the hunt because it makes (the other team) nervous."

We must admit, we didn't see this coming, not this much precision colliding, not this steadily. Some announcers have referred to the big hits as "Kronwallian," an adjective Kronwall shrugs off. Sure, he's happy to hit, happy to have an impact the Wings have craved. But really, he's just happy to be hunting, finally. ●

Red Wings defenseman Niklas Kronwall finished plus–25 this season with 44 PIM.
David Guralnick/The Detroit News

By John Niyo

CHELIOS CHURNING
Extreme training rolls back the years

You arrive in this idyllic setting hoping to find the fountain of youth. Paradise Cove, they call it, and the view from Chris Chelios' beachfront property certainly doesn't argue.

But if you're expecting to see Chelios, the second-oldest active player in major U.S. professional sports, sipping from some restorative spring, you're bound to be disappointed.

"Water?" the Wings' 45-year-old defenseman asks, his lips curling into that familiar sneer. "Nah, that's not how we do it."

And with that, he's off, dodging traffic as he crosses the Pacific Coast Highway on his mountain bike, headed for the coastal sage scrub of Escondido Canyon on the aptly-named Winding Way Trail.

He is flanked by his son, Dean, who celebrated his 18th birthday the night before, and a motley crew of multimillionaires: Laird Hamilton, the world's most famous big-wave surfer; Bill Romanowski, the former NFL star with four Super Bowl rings; and Don Wildman, the 74-year-old founder of Bally Total Fitness.

For the next 90 minutes, they will push and pedal and perspire — no water bottle for Chelios, as promised — in the southern California sun.

Up they climb for more than an hour, churning through a mostly dirt track of switchbacks and swanky hillside estates, sending lizards scurrying and even spooking a deer that goes bounding over a ridge. By the time they reach the top, legs are burning with lactic acid.

"Way to go!" Wildman yells, as Romanowski strains up one final, dusty incline and joins the group under a lonely shade tree. "That's a grind all the way, isn't it? No relief on that ride."

No rest for the weary, either. A few minutes later, the bikers are headed back the way they came, hurtling down the hills toward the ocean. And breakfast.

For Chelios, another day in paradise has only just begun.

Finding an edge

He places his order — an egg-white omelet with chicken and spinach, a side of bacon and dry wheat toast — then tries to explain his recipe for success. You don't survive 23 NHL seasons, more than 1,500 regular-season games, and a record 22 Stanley Cup

Chris Chelios acknowledges the crowd after it was announced in the first period he was the second-oldest person to have played in the NHL, behind only Gordie Howe.

David Guralnick/The Detroit News

playoffs without learning a trick or two.

The first, and most important, he says, was a chance meeting in the early 1990s with T.R. Goodman, who would quickly become his training guru.

Goodman tailors a sport-specific workout for the summer, but it's the circuit training — a nonstop, 60-minute succession of exercises that Chelios swears by and others swear at. (The first time ex-teammate Mathieu Schneider tried it, he vomited.) Even in his mid-40s, Chelios still powers through it like "a machine," Goodman says, adding, "It's his competitiveness; that's the reason he's still willing to do the work that you have to do to sustain yourself."

Especially now that it's so crowded at the Gold's Gym in Venice, California, where Goodman's Pro Sports Camp has collected more than 20 NHL clients, including the Wings' Dan Cleary and Jiri Hudler.

"Even as other guys caught on, it wasn't a big deal, because I was still in my 30s," said Chelios, who has signed six contract extensions since joining the Wings via trade in 1999. "Then it got to the point where guys 20 years younger than me were using the same techniques, and I really didn't feel I had an advantage anymore. But that's when I met Don and Laird."

And finally, he'd met his match.

"I don't know anything about hockey," admitted Hamilton, who, along with his wife — ex-model and pro volleyball star Gabrielle Reece — and 3-year-old daughter, splits his time between Malibu and Hawaii, where he made his name defying death in the waters off Maui's North Shore.

"But with me, my first impression is usually instinctual. You either like 'em or you don't. You can smell it. It's like, why does a dog bark at one person and lick somebody else?"

Hamilton's alpha-male personality quickly accepted Chelios into the pack.

"I just like guys that work hard," said Hamilton. "There's no secret; you just do the work. And there's a certain humility with people like that. That's one of the things I like about Chris. He's a humble guy and he's super-cool. He's comfortable."

The 'Malibu Mob'

He's also a contemporary. At 45, Chelios is twice the age of his youngest teammates in Detroit. But here, he's just one of the boys. Hamilton is 43. Romanowski is 41. Another regular in the "Malibu Mob" is former tennis bad boy John McEnroe, 48. And then, of course, there's Wildman, a veteran of nine Ironman triathlons who's now seated across the table at Coogie's Beach Grill, digging into a bowl of fruit.

"There's maybe 5 percent of the guys in the world his age that are doing the things he's doing," said Chelios, shaking his head. "Probably not even that."

Age is not a number with this group. It's an after-thought, sort of like their celebrity status in Malibu, where nearly everyone is rich or famous — or both. (Today's breakfast is interrupted briefly as former NBA star Reggie Miller stops by the table on his way out with the morning paper.)

"How old a guy is? We're not limited by things like that — we don't stereotype," said Hamilton, who last fall pedaled his bike from London to Paris

— crossing the English Channel on a surfboard along the way — to raise awareness about autism. "My favorite motto is 'victory through attrition.' If you're the last guy standing, you win."

He sits upright and raises his hand in mock victory, saluting an imaginary crowd. It's a pose that reminds one of Chelios back in 2002, taunting the fans in Vancouver with a victory lap en route to Detroit's last Stanley Cup.

"I don't know about like-minded," Chelios said. "What I did is I found some extreme guys and I mixed a little of their mentality with mine. I mean,

they go flying down the hill. I don't. Because there's an element of real danger with what these guys do."

Chelios has seen the footage of some of Hamilton's notorious stunts, including conquering the Teahupo'o break in Tahiti back in 2000 — a feat that cemented his legend in surfing. But more to the point, Chelios also has seen his neighbors torture more than a few weekend warriors over the years.

"Every once in a while, guys will show up and just want to train with them," Chelios said, laughing. "And they'll take 'em and just bury them, then come down here to breakfast and have a good laugh about it ... They really get a kick out of that."

'Almost obsessive'

So does Chelios' wife, Tracee, as she sits on a lounge chair, watching her husband of 20 years wrestle with their two boys, Dean and Jake, in the water. Nearby, Hamilton is busy schooling the Chelios girls, Kaley and Tara, on the finer points of longboard surfing.

"All these guys are a little on the nutty side," Tracee said, nodding. "They're all a little crazy — almost obsessive about it. I mean, working out is like a 9-to-5 job for Chris."

Actually, the workday starts quite a bit earlier than that.

Trouble is, he can't train like he used to. Not after all that wear and tear on his joints, particularly the left knee that underwent reconstructive surgery in 2000. So there's less impact and more strength work involved.

But it's the same 5:45 AM start to his day for circuit training in Venice, then back home for weightlifting in his own gym, followed by the mountain biking. Then, after lunch, he'll jump in the Pacific with his surfboard.

Chris Chelios bikes on Winding Way trail near his home in Malibu, California.
David Guralnick/The Detroit News

"It's all about trying to keep it interesting," Hamilton said, "and keeping you inspired."

Hamilton's latest inspiration is the reincarnation of a centuries-old Hawaiian tradition: paddle surfing. Using an oversized board and a long, outrigger paddle, Chelios joins Hamilton and Wildman for three- and four-hour excursions.

The stand-up paddling style allows them the luxury of catching waves farther from shore, well before the other surfers even get on their feet. And watching the serene but strenuous balancing act from shore, it doesn't take an exercise physiologist to understand the core-strengthening benefits for a hockey player like Chelios, though when asked about it later, he insisted, "It's not better, it's different."

Which makes it better, of course, in a round-about way.

"It sure as hell beats sitting on a stationary bike," Chelios said. "I've found a way to train and have fun."

He's keeping track

A casual conversation turns on a question from out of left field.

"Hey, is Julio Franco still playing for the Mets?" Chelios asked.

When told that New York had waived the 48-year-old first baseman a couple days earlier, Chelios finishes his thought, "I think that makes me the oldest now."

He was right, of course. With Franco gone (although he would later sign with Atlanta), Chelios became the elder statesman of the four major professional sports leagues — Major League Baseball, NFL, NBA, and NHL. But you get the feeling he already knew the answer. So maybe the age does matter?

"I hear that every day now — I've got guys in Detroit and all around the league telling me, 'Keep it up. You're a real inspiration for me, still playing at 45,' " said Chelios, whose NHL Players Association duties also keep him busy during the summer, shuttling back and forth to Toronto for meetings.

"But you know what?" he added, nodding in Wildman's direction. "I wake up every morning and have a guy who's 74 tearing me up like he does. So that's my inspiration."

There's this, too: His eldest son was getting ready to play Tier I junior hockey in the hopes of landing a college scholarship. And to get ready, Dean — a 6'1", 170-pound forward — was training alongside his father this summer.

"He's got to start training a lot harder than he's used to," Chris said. "So that's part of my motivation, too, to try to show my kids the work ethic you have to have."

When will it all end?

"You'd think he'd have gotten sick of it by now, but he doesn't," Tracee said. "Every season is like his first."

Asked if she sees the last on the horizon, Tracee laughed. Might he still be playing at age 50?

"Nothing would surprise me," she said. "If you would've told me 20 years ago he'd still be playing now, I would've said you were crazy. But it's not even an issue anymore. He'll come back and say, 'I signed today,' and I'll be like, 'OK, that's great.'

"It's funny, I always thought I'd get all this help with the kids when he retired. Now I just tell him, 'You might as well keep playing, because I don't need any help now. The kids are all grown up.'"

She laughed again. Her kids have already come back to shore. And it's the grown-ups — Chris and Laird — who are still out in the water, splashing away in the fountain of youth. ●

REGULAR SEASON

DATE	OPPONENT	RESULT	W-L-OL	TOP PERFORMER
Wed, Oct. 3	Anaheim	W 3-2 SO	1-0-0	H. Zetterberg, G: 1, A: 1
Sat, Oct. 6	@Chicago	L 4-3 SO	1-0-1	N. Lidstrom, G: 1, A: 1
Mon, Oct. 8	Edmonton	W 4-2	2-0-1	M. Samuelsson, G: 1, A: 1
Wed, Oct. 10	Calgary	W 4-2	3-0-1	P. Datsyuk, G: 0, A: 2
Fri, Oct. 12	Chicago	L 3-2	3-1-1	H. Zetterberg, G: 1, A: 0
Sun, Oct. 14	@Los Angeles	W 4-1	4-1-1	P. Datsyuk, G: 1, A: 2
Mon, Oct. 15	@Anaheim	L 6-3	4-2-1	H. Zetterberg, G: 1, A: 0
Thu, Oct. 18	@San Jose	W 4-2	5-2-1	B. Rafalski, G: 0, A: 3
Sat, Oct. 20	@Phoenix	W 5-2	6-2-1	K. Maltby, G: 2, A: 0
Wed, Oct. 24	Vancouver	W 3-2	7-2-1	T. Holmstrom, G: 2, A: 0
Fri, Oct. 26	San Jose	W 5-1	8-2-1	H. Zetterberg, G: 2, A: 0
Sun, Oct. 28	@Vancouver	W 3-2	9-2-1	C. Osgood, SV%: 0.93
Tue, Oct. 30	@Edmonton	W 2-1	10-2-1	C. Osgood, SV%: 0.94
Thu, Nov. 1	@Calgary	W 4-1	11-2-1	C. Osgood, SV%: 0.96
Wed, Nov. 7	Nashville	W 3-2 SO	12-2-1	C. Osgood, SV%: 0.93
Fri, Nov. 9	Columbus	W 4-1	13-2-1	D. Cleary, G: 2, A: 0
Sun, Nov. 11	@Chicago	L 3-2	13-3-1	J. Hudler, G: 1, A: 1
Tue, Nov. 13	@St. Louis	L 4-3	13-4-1	N. Kronwall, G: 0, A: 2
Sat, Nov. 17	Chicago	L 5-3	13-5-1	H. Zetterberg, G: 1, A: 1
Sun, Nov. 18	@Columbus	W 5-4 SO	14-5-1	N. Lidstrom, G: 1, A: 2
Wed, Nov. 21	St. Louis	W 3-0	15-5-1	D. Cleary, G: 1, A: 1
Thu, Nov. 22	@Nashville	L 3-2	15-6-1	H. Zetterberg, G: 1, A: 0
Sat, Nov. 24	@Columbus	L 3-2 SO	15-6-2	P. Datsyuk, G: 1, A: 1
Tue, Nov. 27	Calgary	W 5-3	16-6-2	P. Datsyuk, G: 2, A: 1
Thu, Nov. 29	Tampa Bay	W 4-2	17-6-2	D. Cleary, G: 1, A: 0
Sat, Dec. 1	Phoenix	W 3-2	18-6-2	H. Zetterberg, G: 1, A: 1
Tue, Dec. 4	@Montreal	W 4-1	19-6-2	P. Datsyuk, G: 2, A: 1
Fri, Dec. 7	Minnesota	W 5-0	20-6-2	H. Zetterberg, G: 3, A: 3
Sun, Dec. 9	Carolina	W 5-2	21-6-2	J. Hudler, G: 0, A: 3
Mon, Dec. 10	@Nashville	W 2-1	22-6-2	C. Osgood, SV%: 0.97
Thu, Dec. 13	Edmonton	L 4-3 SO	22-6-3	H. Zetterberg, G: 2, A: 0
Sat, Dec. 15	Florida	W 5-2	23-6-3	C. Osgood, SV%: 0.94
Mon, Dec. 17	Washington	W 4-3 SO	24-6-3	H. Zetterberg, G: 1, A: 1
Wed, Dec. 19	Los Angeles	W 6-2	25-6-3	N. Kronwall, G: 0, A: 4
Thu, Dec. 20	@St. Louis	L 3-2	25-7-3	N. Lidstrom, G: 0, A: 1
Sat, Dec. 22	@Minnesota	W 4-1	26-7-3	Hasek D. Cleary, G: 1, A: 1
Wed, Dec. 26	@St. Louis	W 5-0	27-7-3	C. Osgood, SV%: 1.00
Thu, Dec. 27	@Colorado	W 4-2	28-7-3	V. Filppula, G: 2, A: 0
Sat, Dec. 29	@Phoenix	W 4-2	29-7-3	P. Datsyuk, G: 1, A: 2
Mon, Dec. 31	St. Louis	L 2-0	29-8-3	D. Hasek, SV%: 0.96
Wed, Jan. 2	Dallas	W 4-1	30-8-3	C. Osgood, SV%: 0.96
Sat, Jan. 5	@Dallas	W 3-0	31-8-3	D. Hasek, SV%: 1.00
Sun, Jan. 6	@Chicago	W 3-1	32-8-3	C. Osgood, SV%: 0.95
Tue, Jan. 8	Colorado	W 1-0	33-8-3	D. Hasek, SV%: 1.00
Thu, Jan. 10	Minnesota	L 6-5 SO	33-8-4	D. Cleary, G: 1, A: 2
Sat, Jan. 12	@Ottawa	L 3-2	33-9-4	N. Lidstrom, G: 0, A: 1
Tue, Jan. 15	Atlanta	L 5-1	33-10-4	M. Samuelsson, G: 0, A: 1
Thu, Jan. 17	Vancouver	W 3-2 SO	34-10-4	D. Cleary, G: 2, A: 0
Sat, Jan. 19	@San Jose	W 6-3	35-10-4	N. Lidstrom, G: 1, A: 2
Tue, Jan. 22	@Los Angeles	W 3-0	36-10-4	C. Osgood, SV%: 1.00
Wed, Jan. 23	@Anaheim	W 2-1	37-10-4	D. Hasek, SV%: 0.96
Wed, Jan. 30	Phoenix	W 3-2	38-10-4	N. Lidstrom, G: 1, A: 2
Fri, Feb. 1	Colorado	W 2-0	39-10-4	P. Datsyuk, G: 0, A: 2

Date	Opponent	Result	Record	Top Performer
Sat, Feb. 2	@Boston	W 3-1	40-10-4	P. Datsyuk, G: 1, A: 1
Tue, Feb. 5	@Minnesota	W 3-2 OT	41-10-4	D. Cleary, G: 1, A: 1
Thu, Feb. 7	Los Angeles	L 5-3	41-11-4	H. Zetterberg, G: 2, A: 0
Sat, Feb. 9	@Toronto	L 3-2 OT	41-11-5	N. Lidstrom, G: 1, A: 1
Sun, Feb. 10	Anaheim	L 3-2	41-12-5	N. Lidstrom, G: 0, A: 1
Tue, Feb. 12	@Nashville	L 4-2	41-13-5	J. Howard, SV%: 0.95
Fri, Feb. 15	Columbus	L 5-1	41-14-5	P. Datsyuk, G: 1, A: 0
Sun, Feb. 17	@Dallas	L 1-0	41-15-5	J. Howard, SV%: 0.97
Mon, Feb. 18	@Colorado	W 4-0	42-15-5	P. Datsyuk, G: 0, A: 3
Fri, Feb. 22	@Calgary	L 1-0	42-16-5	C. Osgood, SV%: 0.96
Sat, Feb. 23	@Vancouver	L 4-1	42-17-5	D. Meech, G: 0, A: 1
Tue, Feb. 26	@Edmonton	L 4-3 SO	42-17-6	M. Samuelsson, G: 0, A: 1
Fri, Feb. 29	San Jose	L 3-2	42-18-6	H. Zetterberg, G: 1, A: 1
Sun, March 2	@Buffalo	W 4-2	43-18-6	J. Franzen, G: 1, A: 1
Wed, March 5	St. Louis	W 4-1	44-18-6	P. Datsyuk, G: 2, A: 0
Sun, March 9	Nashville	W 4-3	45-18-6	J. Franzen, G: 2, A: 0
Tue, March 11	Chicago	W 3-1	46-18-6	P. Datsyuk, G: 1, A: 0
Thu, March 13	Dallas	W 5-3	47-18-6	P. Datsyuk, G: 2, A: 1
Sat, March 15	Nashville	L 3-1	47-19-6	C. Osgood, SV%: 0.92
Sun, March 16	@Columbus	L 4-3	47-20-6	J. Franzen, G: 2, A: 0
Wed, March 19	Columbus	W 3-1	48-20-6	H. Zetterberg, G: 3, A: 0
Thu, March 20	@Nashville	W 6-3	49-20-6	P. Datsyuk, G: 2, A: 0
Sat, March 22	@Columbus	W 4-1	50-20-6	P. Datsyuk, G: 1, A: 2
Tue, March 25	@St. Louis	W 2-1	51-20-6	C. Osgood, SV%: 0.94
Fri, March 28	St. Louis	L 4-3 OT	51-20-7	H. Zetterberg, G: 0, A: 3
Sun, March 30	Nashville	W 1-0 OT	52-20-7	D. Hasek, SV%: 1.00
Wed, April 2	@Chicago	L 6-2	52-21-7	K. Maltby, G: 1, A: 0
Thu, April 3	Columbus	W 3-2	53-21-7	P. Datsyuk, G: 0, A: 2
Sun, April 6	Chicago	W 4-1	54-21-7	D. Hasek, SV%: 0.96

CONFERENCE QUARTERFINALS

DATE	OPPONENT	RESULT	W-L-OL	TOP PERFORMER
Thu, April 10	Nashville	W 3-1	1-0-0	H. Zetterberg, G: 2, A: 0
Sat, April 12	Nashville	W 4-2	2-0-0	T. Holmstrom, G: 1, A: 1
Mon, April 14	@Nashville	L 5-3	2-1-0	J. Hudler, G: 1, A: 1
Wed, April 16	@Nashville	L 3-2	2-2-0	P. Datsyuk, G: 2, A: 0
Fri, April 18	Nashville	W 2-1 OT	3-2-0	J. Franzen, G: 1, A: 1
Sun, April 20	@Nashville	W 3-0	4-2-0	C. Osgood, SV%: 1.00

CONFERENCE SEMIFINALS

DATE	OPPONENT	RESULT	W-L-OL	TOP PERFORMER
Thu, April 24	Colorado	W 4-3	5-2-0	J. Franzen, G: 2, A: 1
Sat, April 26	Colorado	W 5-1	6-2-0	J. Franzen, G: 3, A: 0
Tue, April 29	@Colorado	W 4-3	7-2-0	P. Datsyuk, G: 2, A: 1
Thu, May 1	@Colorado	W 8-2	8-2-0	H. Zetterberg, G: 2, A: 2

CONFERENCE FINALS

DATE	OPPONENT	RESULT	W-L-OL	TOP PERFORMER
Thu, May 8	Dallas	W 4-1	9-2-0	C. Osgood, SV%: 0.95
Sat, May 10	Dallas	W 2-1	10-2-0	H. Zetterberg, G: 1, A: 0
Mon, May 12	@Dallas	W 5-2	11-2-0	P. Datsyuk, G: 3, A: 0
Wed, May 14	@Dallas	L 3-1	11-3-0	H. Zetterberg, G: 1, A: 0
Sat, May 17	Dallas	L 2-1	11-4-0	P. Datsyuk, G: 0, A: 0
Mon, May 19	@Dallas	W 4-1	12-4-0	C. Osgood, SV%: 0.97

STANLEY CUP FINALS

DATE	OPPONENT	RESULT	W-L-OL	TOP PERFORMER
Sat, May 24	Pittsburgh	W 4-0	13-4-0	C. Osgood, SV%: 1.00
Mon, May 26	Pittsburgh	W 3-0	14-4-0	C. Osgood, SV%: 1.00
Wed, May 28	@Pittsburgh	L 3-2	14-5-0	J. Franzen, G: 1, A: 0
Sat, May 31	@Pittsburgh	W 2-1	15-5-0	C. Osgood, SV%: 0.96
Mon, June 2	Pittsburgh	L 4-3 OT	15-5-1	H. Zetterberg, G: 0, A: 2
Wed, June 4	@Pittsburgh	W 3-2	16-5-1	H. Zetterberg, G: 1, A: 1